THE GOOI

10 STEPS TO GET

SCHOOL

BY **KK HARRIS**

Acknowledgments

To say I could have gotten this book out to the world on my own would be telling a lie. I am a super woman but we all need friends and I have some fantastic friends and family that have supported me over the last year to help me get the book done. They didn't write it with me but they were there in their own special way so I want to give them the respect that is due. So here we go.

Firstly I have to thank my daughter Ty, my official case study. My little nugget of love, who is an inch plus taller than me now, you complete me. "You complete me" is a line from a film that was before your time, but I think it sums up how having you as my daughter has given me so much and helped me grow in ways that I continue to explain a bit at a time. I don't want to scare you about my past. Lol. You rock honey. I am so proud of how you went for it during your exams and smashed it and achieved as well as you did.

Andrea Deighton, you have shown me the joys of using a flip chart. Thanks for being there as I neared the finish line and thanks for being a pair of editing eyes.

Amanda, sis you literally got me to get the book done. It was during the last mile, in my marathon of writing this book that you gave me one final shout "C'mon Karime finish it!" Thank you for seeing me for who I am and understanding I was never meant for a 9-5.

Ed "Big Daddy", you are literally a rock in our untraditional family. Ty is awesome because of you too. You have always been and will always be there for our Ty and for that I am proud to say I co-parent with a great guy. Thanks for constantly supporting me through all that I do. I appreciate you.

Jane DeCroos, another fabulous woman that showed me the importance of sticking to a schedule and planning for delays. Plus you do have the greatest chilli sauce on the planet called Chilli Drops. People go to her website to order yours at **www.chillidrops.co.uk**

To all my siblings, Felicia, Ken (my twin) Lee, Amanda, Romarque, Kevin, Trevor, Sheridan, Sheryl, (the other twins) and Genii (my sister in my soul) I want you to know just because I live in the UK doesn't mean I don't think of you, I do everyday. Thank God for Facebook!

To my Dad Kent Harris, you have shown me, through example, how to keep growing and moving forward. I am who I am today because of who you are and how you live, changing where necessary, never giving up. Never using your age as an excuse to sit and do nothing. I am so proud to be your daughter and to be so much like you. I love you dad.

Contributors

Special thanks goes to Chad Kunego for laying out my book so beautifully and for being patient with me. I keep opening the pages with a smile because as a lover of the written word, the layout has to be right honey and you made sure mine is. Thank you again. I look forward to starting the next project with you.

Special thanks to Keri Lam for designing a fantastic front and back cover! It's timeless. You really are a rock star.

Jennifer Stoute I am in gratitude to have been able to interview you for my book. You gave me more of your time than expected. You are one heck of a business- woman and mother. Thank you again.

Kanako Wakatsuki-Hobbs you came into our lives like a gift from Heaven. Because of your influence our Ty has truly developed into a pianist. Thank you so much for your contribution to my book and our lives. I will miss you whilst you are away for six months in Hong Kong but lessons will continue via Skype, so once you're settled, see you on the laptop.

Julia Keller thank you for being a supporter and contributor to my mission to help other parent's and their children to achieve a top education that I believe all children deserve. It's always a giggle when we get together. Maybe I'll slow down enough to find love through the help of your Love Coaching services. Julia can be reached at **juliakellercoaching@gmail.com**

Seth and Delia of the Hampstead Dyslexia Clinic in London, you two are such incredible individuals with huge hearts. I learned so much about Dyslexia that I didn't know. ☺Thank you for giving your time so freely.

Note to other self-publishers:

Contact Chad Kunego for book layout at:

business@whatthepublishing.com
www.whatthepublishing.com

Contact Keri Lam for your cover design at:

lam.cmkeri@gmail.com

Contents

INTRODUCTION

I know you've been hearing stories about friends of friends' children not getting an offer from top secondary schools they applied to. Or how the child has been put on the waiting list and is way down past hope on the list. All you keep hearing is how difficult it is to get your child a place at a top school and as your child is approaching year five you are finding tension in your shoulders you've never had before.

I bet you wish someone would tell you it isn't really that bad. Well I wish I could lie to you but I can't because it's true. It isn't an easy task these days especially if you live in a major city like London, where schools have reported receiving 1100 applications for less than 90 places. It's insane but again it's true. As you hear other moms talking about the process it sounds so scary and it makes you feel like it might not be in your son or daughter's future.

Set those fears aside because there is a guide that will help you to prepare your child for school entrance exams, the personal interview process and the scholarship and bursary application and it is this book that you are reading right now. I have put together this 10- step guide to get your child into a top school. Without insider knowledge how would anyone know how to go about the whole process? You wouldn't. You would be depending on second, third and fourth-hand information that will only leave you stressed out and confused. You don't ever have to be in the land of the unknown again as long as you let this book be your guide.

I am a mother just like you. I have a darling daughter who has gone through the Common Entrance Exams recently and so I know first hand the anxiety that accompanies the whole process. I felt like the ex-pat I am, alone in a foreign land with no one to hold my hand and show me the way. Suddenly, the other mothers were too busy to have coffee and play dates ended as soon as year 5 started. I asked questions to anyone that would listen and who had been through it years before. Sometimes it made me feel worse. Compound that with the fact that I didn't have the money for my child to get a private school education. I was divorced and was a full time student in university. The odds were completely against us. But with my support, my daughter had earned a bursary place at a private London primary school, so I knew it was possible.

There is one thing friends will say about me, and that is "KK is driven to find a way through any barrier!" There was no way I was going to let the fact that I was broke and not British stop my daughter from getting a top secondary education. I'm pleased to share that she didn't get just one acceptance letter but SHE GOT THREE! Plus she earned two art scholarships!

My daughter is not a genius and she'd rather be playing with her Ever After High dolls or building in Minecraft instead of practicing piano or doing homework. Sound familiar? One thing she learned through the whole process is how to work hard to achieve goals that seem unreachable and I learned the same thing. Her hard work was accompanied by my gentle and sometimes firm guidance. In this book I give you the same strategy so you can achieve the same end result, GET YOUR CHILD INTO A TOP SCHOOL. The same strategy that has my phone ringing off the hook with mums, just like you, wanting to hire me as their personal consultant to help guide them personally, for which I am truly privileged to do.

I promise that if you just put into action the 10 steps in this book then you will be able to get your child into a top school. I have done it. Other women like you are doing it too. By purchasing this book you are one step closer to realising your dream of a great education for your child. Don't be the mum that doesn't read this book but wishes she had when her child doesn't get a place in a top school.

All it takes is for you to start by reading **Step 1. Building Your Childs CV**, which is so crucial for the application. I explain what its all about and how to put it all together in the book. I will take you step-by-step, leaving no stone unturned, through the process. Inside you'll find a section called **Interviews**, which really is a good read. I interviewed Jennifer Stoute, female 1992 British Olympian Bronze Medal winner of the 400m Relay. She gives her insights on supporting her teenage daughter who went from a weighty ten year old to becoming a British Number One Junior athlete and what it takes as a parent to support a sports star. If you suspect your child may have Dyslexia then you'll be interested to read the interview of the clinicians/owners of the Hampstead Dyslexia Clinic in London. I have also interviewed Kanako Watkatsuki, Japanese concert pianist and private piano teacher who has helped children prepare for ABRSM piano exams and scholarship auditions.

Kids love to have fun and as a mum I know this to be true. So I've made the process fun as well. Like in **Chapter 8. Interview Skills**, I suggest you and your child create an interview project that will be fun and give your child something talk about, which will alleviate nerves. I know you will enjoy this guide and find it useful and I hope that you will share it and like it on your social media pages.

This book is something I wrote because I know what you are going through. I promised myself that if I could get my daughter into a top secondary school then I would write this book for women like me that just needed a helping hand to put their best foot forward. That helping hand is extended out to you in the 10 Steps to Get Your Child into Top School. It's all here and I'm so excited that you have purchased it and are taking action by using my proven strategy that changed my daughter's future and will do the same for your darling son or daughter too.

I'm an educational consultant so do get in touch for a free twenty minute initial consultation so we can discuss how I can help you on your journey. You can email me on **goodmumsguide@gmail.com**

KK Harris

ABOUT THE AUTHOR

KK (actual name Karime Kendra) Harris was born and raised in Los Angeles California. She has a twin brother and nine other half brothers and sisters. Her father is Northern Soul songwriter and producer Kent Harris. Her mother is the late singer and Northern Soul darling Ty Karim.

KK made London her permanent home in 1999. She has one child, a daughter, named Ty who she named after her mother. Ty is eleven years old and attends Christ's Hospital School in England. KK calls herself a super-mom with serious skills in multi-tasking. She has maintained an excellent co-parenting relationship with her ex-husband, which she believes is the reason her daughter is so adjusted and not full of angst.

KK is author of a book called "I Don't Want to Be a Chicken Nugget!" She also produced and voiced the audio book version, which she gives to her tutoring clients. It's a story about two chickens that plan an escape from the farm to avoid being sent to the city to become chicken nuggets. When asked if it was a statement book against McDonalds, KK laughed and responded, "No. It's a book about friendship and not listening to rumours."

Along side of being an author KK Harris is a qualified Montessori Kindergarten teacher. She also holds a certificate in Psychoanalytic Psychology from Birkbeck University in London. She will graduate with a degree in Accounting & Finance from Plymouth University in 2016. Asked if she'll do another degree and KK replied, "I think I've done enough, but I will start taking piano lessons soon because I have a grand piano that will need attention during the weeks Ty is away at boarding school."

KK spent over twenty years in the music business as a professional singer and songwriter known as Karime Kendra. She's sang throughout Europe, Sweden, Russia and even found out she was pregnant with her daughter whilst on tour in Istanbul, Turkey. She gave up the microphone in 2011 when her mother in law, and well- known artist, Gale Pitt died. She knew she would have to be there for her daughter during a time of such great lost. Her mother died when she was a teen so she knew how confusing it would be for Ty who was only seven at the time. KK was also grieving. She said that the loss of Gale felt like losing a second mother. She walked away from the music industry without regret. She does say she feels like singing live again these days but just for the love of it and not as a career.

KK has developed a mentoring program for secondary school students and women called Change180. She and her business partner Andrea intend to launch the program in the UK in 2016. She says it's her "legacy project". The program is aimed to empower young people and women to change their lives and not be defined by their past mistakes or the labels other's have placed on them. KK has a chequered past but has found a way to release the old and embrace a new her and to raise a healthy daughter along the way. She knows the life she lives is an example of how it is possible to do a Change180 and create a life worth living.

KK is a breath of fresh air. She brings to the table an interesting past of wild behaviour, pain and hardship. She has a tattoo of her late mother on her right arm. Her smile is big in that Julia Roberts kind of way. She also has amazing straight teeth that only Americans seem to have. When she sits with you it's her voice that makes you instantly relax, feeling as if you've known her forever. She's very easy to talk to. I brought my six-year old daughter along to meet her and the reaction by Gabriella was quite sweet. She insisted on sitting next to KK so she could show her all the pictures she was drawing for her. As I sit in the presence of this very intriguing woman called KK Harris, I'm happy that I know her and I'm confident we'll be friends to come for many years.

J. Keller

STEP 1: BUILDING YOUR CHILD'S CV

"Success depends upon previous preparation, and without such preparation there is sure to be failure." Confucius

I know what you're thinking "my child isn't applying for a job!" and you are right they aren't but you are applying to schools that want to know more about them than just how smart they are. Don't get me wrong, how well your child does on their exams is highly important, but by building a CV that showcases other facets of your child it will help to boost his/her application. It also helps during the personal interview that most private schools require either before the exam or after. The interview is really a great opportunity for your child to shine. It's when they can share what they like doing outside of school and any team sports they may be involved in. If your son or daughter has a funny personality the Head Teacher or Principal will be able to pick up on that and make a note about their awesome sense of humour.

The key to a good CV for your child is preparation and without it you'll be scurrying at the last minute to find ways to hep your child feel confident during interviews. If your child is nervous about the interview because they don't know what to expect then they won't do well and that is bad. The more prepared your child is, the more confidence they exude in any unknown situation.

How you put together a CV for your ten-year-old is similar to putting one together for a job. So, with pen in hand this is what I want you to do. I want you to open up a notebook and at the top of a piece of paper write down your son or daughter's name. Then create headings for columns titled 1. Music 2. Art 3. Drama. 4. Sports. 5. Dance. After that start listing any activities they participate in that fall under each heading. If they play the flute put it under Music and so on and so forth. This really shouldn't take but a minute or so.

I want you to be critical when looking at the list. Ask yourself what on this list are they really passionate about? Not your passion but theirs. I know I wanted my daughter to really get into gymnastics and be one of those girls doing back flips all over the place, but that was my dream. My daughter was not interested in the balance beam and was seriously afraid of falling so that wasn't happening. For a long time I was taking my daughter to Saturday gymnastics club out of habit and my own desires, so when I said enough is enough she was over the moon and happy to be splashing in the pool instead. After she got through the fear and gained her badge (we never give up) we settled on swimming for her sport of choice. So, casting your dreams aside put a star only next to the activities they are really interested in and would love to be doing every day without complaint. You will probably have one to three things on the list. Anymore than that then you must be exhausted running them around to clubs and I imagine your night ends with a glass of red. Lol.

You've put your list together and now what I want you to do is to eliminate any activities that do not have a star by it. Yes, I want you to stop going to those activities. You are going to have a chat with your child and tell them "its time to focus on your favourite activities". When a child isn't really interested in something, they are happy when they don't have to do it anymore. Besides you'll realise that you were probably doing those activities robotically. Please don't get emotionally tied into the coffee you'll miss having with the ladies you've met there. We are on a mission here and that is to GET YOUR CHILD INTO A TOP SCHOOL. Arrange to have a coffee some other time.

Make sure you cancel with the club and cancel your direct debit. Always take care of business first. If they are in the middle of the term either pull them right out and never look back or wait until the end of term. It really is up to you but bear in mind that if little George isn't waking up wanting to play Rugby then he isn't going to mind stopping before the end of term. By pulling him out early you will be saving time, which is undoubtedly in short supply. You'll also make time to add another day of an activity that your child is really excited about and is talented in. Be ruthless and cut those time-wasting clubs.

Your child's CV on paper should reflect who they are and not who you want them to be. I don't want you to think that you have to type up their club list and attach it to the application. I just call it a CV because that's how I need you to picture it as something that is just as important because it is. Within the school application you will be asked to write down any other information regarding your child that you think they should know. Bear this in mind as you go through the different steps in the book.

STEP 2: THE 10K HOUR RULE

"I believe that we learn by practice. Whether it means to learn to dance by practicing dancing or to learn to live by practicing living, the principles are the same. In each, it is the performance of a dedicated precise set of acts, physical or intellectual, from which comes shape of achievement, a sense of one's being, a satisfaction of spirit. One becomes, in some area, an athlete of God. Practice means to perform, over and over again in the face of all obstacles, some act of vision, of faith, or desire. Practice is a means of inviting the perfection desired."
- Martha Graham

Have you heard of the 10,000-hour rule to becoming an expert? People have done studies to discover what it takes to be a top athlete or musician, for example, and what was discovered is that along with certain things like being in the right place to meet the right coaches etc, that it takes 10,000 hours to become a pro at anything. I read a book called 'Bounce' by Matthew Syed, which broke it all down. With that rule in mind I had my daughter build up to a 90 minute piano practice and in less than two years she took her Grade 5 and achieved a Merit. Everyone thought she must be a child prodigy, but the fact is that she simply practiced three times more than her friends who had been playing for around 4 years. It is simple maths and dedication from both the parent and child. By adding an additional class of your son or daughter's favourite activity then you will be helping your child reach a higher level of ability much faster. Practice is what's going to be needed if you are going to be applying for scholarships for your child.

One day my daughter said to me that one of her classmates said, "Scholarships are for poor people". My jaw fell open and I thought that her classmate had obviously heard this from an adult but of course I can't be sure. For months we had been spending time preparing for scholarships in both art and music and I didn't want my child to feel like she was poor because she was aiming for a scholarship. I believe you can have a bank account with six figures but be poor in spirit or health. So this is what I said to my hard working daughter to squash that negative attitude toward scholarships.

Scholarships are not for poor people. They are for those that have achieved a standard that is higher than the average. It is about prestige and comes with great respect from the school as well as from the public. When you let anyone know your child has been offered a scholarship, the admiration and dare I say it, envy is written all over his or her face. They know that there must have been some serious commitment going on for the child to have achieved such an accolade. A scholarship gives the child the opportunity to work with say the Director of Music at the school or the Artist in Residence. The Sports coach will be taking little George under his wing to develop his athletic abilities. It's really exciting. It also means that there are opportunities to perform for the school in concerts as a soloist or the lead in a dramatic production.

At some schools a discount of 20% off school fees apply to the scholarship award. At other schools it's just about the prestige. Some schools will even add a bursary with the award if you can't pay the fees, but not all schools offer this. If you are going to go for a scholarship remember the competition will be fierce. In music, a lot of schools want the children to have gained a Grade 4 at Distinction on their first instrument, and will require a second instrument, of which the voice can be considered I wish someone had told me about this criteria earlier because I would have been on it a couple of years before. I had to tell my daughter weeks before her music auditions that she would have to sing. Luckily, with the help of her music teacher we were able to get her mentally and vocally ready for her audition.

This leads me to **preparation**. You have put together the list and you are now focused only on what your child is good at. If your daughter is good at singing, drama and dance then please support her by enrolling her into a weekend Stage Coach or somewhere like Sylvia Young in central London. They have weekend programmes that will develop your child's craft. They usually have a big production that they will be working towards during the year. You can then add this to the   scholarship application when asked "Has your child taken part in any productions either at school or professionally?" You'll also be asked for references from their teachers. The more you can write on the application the more weight it will have, and the greater the chance you'll have of those in charge of the scholarships putting a star next to your child's name.

If you find the expense too beefy at certain performance schools, then look for local theatre groups. Look online on free sights like Gumtree. Small companies are always advertising their new businesses. Word of caution though, make sure you enquire how long they have been in business and if they do any end of year performances. You don't want to end up with a company that is going out of business or doesn't understand the importance of end of year shows. If you simply research for an hour or so one evening, there is no reason you shouldn't have a list of 3-5 clubs to phone or

E-mail the following day. Then go and have a visit. Request a free session. If they are doing god business then they'll have no reason to say no. That goes for any activities you are looking to get your child into. A good reputable business will be more than happy to give your child a taster session. So go for it.

Art schools are a great way to develop a standout portfolio for your child. Once again the private schools will ask for references, so you need someone on side. Hampstead School of Art runs some fabulous programmes on the weekend for kids. My daughter went there. She took drawing classes and pottery. We actually took a family class together which created a stronger bond and I really enjoyed learning drawing techniques. It was time on a Sunday where we just focused for two hours on art and it was really relaxing. Being a student also gave me access to private tutors that I could ask questions about putting together a strong art portfolio.

Please look online to find local or national art competitions for your child to take part in. My daughter took part in quite a few and won two big competitions with Aardman Studios for her plasticine models of Wallace and Gromit film characters. I'm telling you she was so proud to show off her signed certificate to friends, family and her teachers at school. She placed it into her portfolio and showed it off during her art scholarship auditions, making a very good impression. Like the cover of my book states, my daughter earned two scholarships and both were in Art. Please take my advice.

If your child is a keen athlete and has opportunities to play on a local team or is a talented tennis player, for example, then be prepared for weekly competitions and practice either before school or after. I know an awesome mum to a talented tennis player. She was her son's driver to every competition and practice. She juggled his sporting life with her own studies when she had gone back to university to study full time. She said she used the two hours he practiced to study for her exams and write her university papers. I have so much respect for her. Her and her son's dedication paid off. He earned a sport's scholarship at a top boarding school and all the while she maintained her scholarship at her university. Anything is possible when you set your mind to it.

Schools like to see outside participation in competitions because it not only tells them something about your child but it also says a lot about who you are and the support you give your child.

Practice -Practice –Practice is the key to excellence. If you and your child are not willing to sit down and put in the time necessary to achieve a high level on an instrument or commit to playing their favourite sport nearly everyday then why would you expect your child to achieve the high level needed to even apply for the scholarships? Scholarships are super competitive, and your child must love the thing they are going for because when he or she loves the activity they'll be asking you if they can put in more time practicing. Remember there is no guarantee that they'll get the scholarship, but it's nice to be considered and it looks really good to the Head Teacher or Principal when the academic results are in and they are deciding on who to offer places to. Imagine you being in the Principal or Bursar's position, if it came down to a final place and you had an applicant who had went out for a scholarship versus one that was just about the academics, who would you choose? I know I would choose the one that had more going on.

I never claimed the journey would be easy. This is a two-way street. Mum, you are going to have to be right there with them during piano practice. If you don't have an ear for music, don't worry; your presence is needed for encouragement. Many a night I prepared dinner or hung the laundry while my daughter practiced. I praised her when it sounded good and supported her when she got frustrated and nudged her to continue. When we are involved they will stay engaged, but as soon as we slip up by letting them not practice, then we are dropping the ball. My daughter's piano teacher, who is a concert pianist, said even she didn't always want to practice when she was a child, but she did it because her mom insisted, and today she is phenomenal. So hang in there. When your son or daughter is playing a piece by Bach or Burgmueller, it will melt your heart.

The same type of support is needed across the board. The more you are able to be there the better. Children are funny, they may not want you to be peering into the room while they practice their dance routine, but they want to know afterwards you were there. They'll usually ask something like,

"Did you see me when I did my arabesque?" You may not even know what an arabesque is, but you better had seen it or you'll have an upset pre-teen on your hands. It's all about support.

The road to creating a nice CV is actually a lot of fun, just as long as you have eliminated activities that aren't necessary and focus on what your child loves to do. Your child will be more than happy to practice and learn new skills. Their confidence will soar. And he or she may earn a coveted scholarship, wouldn't that be nice? At the very least your darling child will have an application that says a lot more about them as a whole person, and that's what the majority of the schools will be looking for. The interview will allow your child to answer questions about what they do outside of school. When a child has more than one feather in their hat then he will able to talk about himself quite easily. So, go for it! And most importantly enjoy the journey with your lovely son or daughter. The time you put it will be a memory to last a lifetime.

Step 3: All you need is love

"Hugs can do great amounts of good, especially for children"
- Princess Diana of Wales

This has to be my best step in the whole book. We were born through love, and with that love your child will be successful in gaining a place at a private school. Preparing to take exams is not easy. Sometimes it's going to be very frustrating, especially for 10 or 11 year olds who would rather be watching Adventure Time on Nickelodeon.

Your child is going to need hugs and cuddles as well as reassurance. If your child attends a very academic school like my daughter, then your son or daughter is going to feel added pressure to achieve high results, because the school is depending on your child to keep their reputation strong. This is how they charge their fees. It's how they make the fees they charge.

I made a point to always give my daughter loads of cuddles, love and encouragement when she had a bad day at school. There were times when she just didn't want to go to school the next day. And there were times when she cried and felt really low. I remember one morning I woke up and said to her, "You know what, you aren't going to school today. We are having a mommy-daughter day. " If you could have heard the exclamations out of her mouth you would have been smiling too. We went out to the park and got on a Barclays bike. I helped my darling girl learn how to ride it with confidence. She had gotten rusty after growing too tall for her old bike. So we spent time laughing as she tried to maneuver her way around people, dogs and pigeons without hurting herself. It was incredible. She was so happy when she managed it, and I felt like she was 6 years old again learning to ride a bike for the first time. She had the biggest grin on her face. When she returned to school the next day, she was a cheery girl and couldn't wait to see her friends to tell them all about her day off.

As parents we have to do the best for our children. I knew missing one day of school was not the end of the world. It actually uplifted her. I'm not telling you that you should pull your child out of school, but it was just to share with you how love and support goes a long way. That day out of school made for a week of smiles, and she gave me loads of kisses, which made me feel wonderful.

When your child brings home a school report, most of us tend to comment on the negative things first. I'm ashamed to share that I did. My smiley gorgeous little girl would suddenly be wearing an upside-down frown on her face. I'm happy to say I changed my behavior. I focused on all the good things the teacher wrote about her progress. At times I never mentioned any negatives. I praised her when the teacher mentioned that her creative writing had gotten better. I gave her high-fives when I read that she got 20/20 for five straight weeks on her mental arithmetic tests. I'm from Los Angeles so you can imagine there was a lot of hooping and hollering going on too.

I got her dad in on the support and praise as well. I would text him any time she told me something great that happened at school so he would be in the loop. He would phone her, and praise her for her achievements no matter how small. Remember a gold star may seem small to us, but to a child it's a big deal. So throw your hands up and ask for a high five. They love it and it feels good.

Me, my daughter and her father may not live together as a traditional family, yet we are a family. It's really important, especially during the build up to exams, for all hands to be on deck. If you don't have a traditional family where both parents are living under the same roof, then any opportunity you can get to do stuff as a family please grab it. Birthdays and half term holidays are perfect times to let the past lie and be a unit that sticks together. If you can put your own issues aside for a few hours to have a meal together then do it for your child and have a pizza on a Friday night after work. Trust me it makes big difference to our children's confidence. Funny thing is that at the schools my daughter attended, other parents had no idea we weren't together, and that was because we both attended her school events and open day's. It's pretty clear that our daughter doesn't have abandonment issues, which will make for a happy teenager in the not too distant future.

I really love being a parent because you get so much in return. Helping to prepare your child for exam time will definitely bring you closer together. You'll find yourself looking back at the past with fondness. One of the things I miss most was the bedtime routine of reading picture books like

Maisy or Charlie and Lola books when my daughter was younger. When she got into reading chapter books it all changed. Even though, I relished being able to go to bed without having to read "The Hungry Caterpillar" five times in a row, fast-forward five years later, I realized that I missed the closeness of that time. During prep we were so exhausted that she often went to bed a bit bummed out because time had run out. I clocked this, and thought 'I want her happy and excited about her future and going into year 7 at a top school', so, I decided that I would read a bit of her chapter book before bedtime, and guess what? She loved it! Turns out she had missed it too. If you don't read to your son or daughter at bedtime anymore then I suggest that you start doing it. Yes at ten or eleven years old they still love hearing you read to them. It's comforting I guess and you'll cherish the memories. They will be adding more to their memory bank to extract from when they are parents themselves. Not only are they preparing for exams, but, they are becoming young ladies and young men and that is a difficult time. My daughter says her friends don't admit that they still play with dolls. So the peer pressure is on to grow up. Reading to your child before bed allows them the freedom to stay young and for us to hold on a bit longer.

You're going to hate me for this next statement but here goes. Why not let your child stay in bed with you some nights. I know it might be uncomfortable but one night is not going to kill you and the result is a big cheesy grin on their face. I'm a sucker for a big hug or smile from my daughter. If you are afraid of getting an elbow in the eye then do what I did and that is put a pillow between you. For some reason unconsciously it stopped her from crossing the barrier. It might work for you. Regardless a night of slight discomfort in exchange for a happy start to the day for your son or daughter is worth it.

Be interested in more than just the academics and activities they are doing. Why not sit down and watch cartoons with them after school. I don't do it all the time but I do make it a point to close my laptop for half an hour and chill with my daughter. Remember, we won't get these days back so why not enjoy them before the teen years begin when they won't think we're cool anymore. Plus, watching cartoons is pretty funny these days. I find I'm laughing hysterically at shows like 'Phineas and Ferb' or 'The Amazing World of Gumball'. The writers really have a great sense of humor. As adults, we need to be able to laugh. Life is hard enough so why not encourage our children to keep laughing, no matter how old they become.

Get out and about on the weekend or after school. Go to your local park and just let him or her run around. Imagine being stuck in school all day with a short break here and there. Remember how it felt when the school bell rang and it was time to leave your jail-that's what it felt like to me. Living in London most children also have the added discomfort of wearing a school uniform with a tie or long sleeve white shirt with fiddly buttons on the cuff. All our kids want to do is be free and who can blame them. Even as I write this I'm telling myself that more fun must be had, starting today! So get out there and enjoy life, because trust me, it will make all the difference along the journey to exam day in January of year 6.

Mom's need love too. I want to talk about loving yourself because you are your son or daughter's example. When I started this journey I was a bit of a wreck. I was in school full-time and money was really tight. My attitude was full of fear. Fearful, that, my darling daughter might not get into a private school. Fearful, that, I didn't have it in me to stay on track. The list went on and on and I began to look tired and mentally drained. I wasn't dating much and I seldom went out with my girlfriends. I was allowing myself to drink more than two drinks on a night out to get to a place where I could just forget about it all. What I didn't realize was that "I wasn't loving me". All the love I had was put into my child. It wasn't until I met my mentor did I come to acknowledge the lack of love I had for myself. When I accepted that I needed to change, then and only then did I begin to enjoy the process of helping my daughter aim for the stars. Our relationship that was already strong got even stronger. I began to really listen to what she had to say instead of nodding my head whilst looking at my Iphone. I let the fear go and found faith in myself. The same faith that I had given my daughter, and you know what? When I started loving me, my daughter found freedom to let her light shine brighter with even more confidence. We laugh way more than ever before.

I can't stress enough about the importance of taking care of you. If you don't look after you, then how will you be able to look and care for that beautiful child of yours? It will be difficult- trust me.

You are probably thinking, it's easier said than done to get motivated to change how you treat yourself. I would argue that it is actually easier than you think. You just have to make the decision to fall in love with yourself. By doing the fun stuff with your child you will notice you are having a good time too. You'll find yourself smiling at the beauty of a flower in the park that your child will give to you. Children are wonderful in that they respond to us with so much love when they see us loving ourselves. Often my daughter is excited when she sees me smiling and laughing. Love is infectious. Her father is happy to see me happy when he drops by. My joy makes him happy to do me a favor when I need a hand with something. The happier you are, the happier your family will be. So please take time to love you. All you have to do is make the decision that you will love yourself everyday.

The love you exude will mean big gains for your son or daughter. I want you to realize there will be a knock-on affect that will happen as a result of you loving yourself more. The love you give to yourself will cancel many disagreements at home. You will see how differently your child will respond to your requests of him/her doing their homework. When I remind my daughter to do her homework with a smile on my face then she smiles and says, "ok" in a sweet tone and gets to it. She is simply reflecting back what she is receiving from me. And oh what a happy home I have as a result. Don't get it twisted, there are moments when my happy tone and requests are met with a "aw, but I was doing something, can I have five more minutes?" My daughter is good at trying to negotiate new terms, which I used to let annoy me but now I just giggle because she's a kid for goodness sakes so she has to test the boundaries. Usually I hear her out, and calmly remind her she has work to do and when she's done she can carry on with whatever she was doing. What I get in return is a girl who gets her work done and gets to have a bit of fun afterwards.

When you are living life in a loving place then you will meet people that are willing to help you along the journey to Get Your Child Into a Top School. People will be drawn to you. Your child's teachers will be more than willing to see you more than once a term because you are a pleasure to have around. I'm telling you, my daughter's year six teacher was awesome. Her school is very English, in that they don't hand out hugs very often to parents, but because of the way I carried myself, her teacher gave me more than a few hugs when I needed them during the final few months of entrance exam preparation. People love happy people and kids love happy parents. I call it operating on a high frequency. And when I'm operating on that higher frequency my daughter responds wonderfully to it.

On a particular occasion I had to acknowledge that I needed to share the housekeeping load with my then ten-year-old daughter. I had struggled with that because I thought she's just a kid and it's my job. When I started to love myself I came to realize that my daughter would be gaining so much by helping out and that I would be doing her a disservice by not teaching her living skills. I also knew that if I was to keep going at the pace I was going at, then I was going to wear myself out. I was in school full-time around 4 days per week and working part-time cleaning and as a PA. I just couldn't do it all. I needed a hand. So I asked her to do the dishes and sweep the floor after dinner. She didn't grumble and she was actually very receptive to the idea. I had asked in a loving manner telling her how I could really use her help around the flat. She could see that it was a request and not an order and that she was actually needed. The result was beyond what I expected. The kitchen was spotless and the next morning when I walked into the kitchen I felt so happy. I praised her so much and gave her loads of morning cuddles. It was great. The love I exuded in my request was met with love from her to me and it was reflected in the job she did.

I could go on and on about the importance of the love and support you give your child and yourself, but I won't because I think you get that I'm big on love. Lol. Love is really all you need.

STEP 4: ACADEMIA

"Excellence is an art won by training and habituation. We do not act rightly because we have virtue or excellence, but we rather have those because we have acted rightly. We are what we repeatedly do. Excellence, then, is not an act but a habit." - Aristotle

It is time to knuckle down and start looking at your child's Math's and English skills. Not only that, but you'll need to assess their Verbal and Non-Verbal Reasoning aptitude. I know this is the boring stuff, which also gives us more stress but the majority of private schools will be looking at the exam results before anything else.

The first port of call is your son or daughter's teacher. You need to schedule in an appointment as soon as possible to discuss any concerns you have. This will also put you in good stead with the teacher because they love knowing that you are on board, especially if your child attends a private primary school. Private schools want nothing more than for your child to go onto earn a place at a good private secondary school. The reason is not because your child deserves it or because they do, but because the schools have a reputation to uphold and if their students don't get into good schools then guess who gets the blame? The primary school does, and parents will pass that negative information on to other parents they know looking for schools, warning them to look elsewhere. Reputation is the name of the game in the private sector. But too much focus on rumors of a schools reputation is also something that can trip you up when applying to secondary schools, which I'll go over in **Step 6 School Selection**.

When you meet with the form teacher, sit down and ask questions about your child's progress and ask if they think there are any specific areas that you should be concerned about. Let him or her know that you are starting to prepare your child for the entrance exams. Also ask if she has any resources available that you can take home, or titles of resources you can purchase online or at your local Waterstones. Take notes. Please arrive with prepared questions and write down the teacher's responses. I know in the past, I have left school meetings without remembering much of what was said. The time you have with your child's teacher is precious and limited so be sure to make the most of it.

Resources are going to be the thing that saves you money in the long run. I know I like saving money and I'm sure you do as well. One great place to start, which always has prep books you can either borrow or copy pages from, is the Library. If you haven't found yourself in a library since your child was in nursery then now is the time to make the effort again. Ask the Librarian about what resources they have. You can always ask them to order other titles too. I find that Librarians are generally very helpful and knowledgeable about the resources it has pertaining to the 11+ prep books they have on the shelf, and will gladly give you a text or call when a book comes in that you ordered if you have been nice and polite.

Have you heard of Bond books and papers? If you haven't then look Bond up online and get excited. These little books are filled with assessment papers, mocks tests and online practice questions that prepare your child for the 11+. They are fairly priced usually costing nothing more than the amount of a Grande Latte and a Croissant. For a monthly subscription price of £5.99 (at time of print) you and your child will have unlimited access to thousands of 11+ practice questions.

I found them to be very useful throughout her primary school education. The books are well designed and there is even an answer booklet that you can pull out to use and correct your son or daughter's work. Bond makes it even easier by creating parental supplements to help you understand how the books work too. But, honestly I found them super easy to use. I believe your child should be doing a minimum of three papers per week as they work toward exams. Oh and the subjects covered are Math, English, Comprehension, Verbal and Non-verbal Reasoning, all the subjects that are on the exams they will sit in January of year 6. These are the subjects you'll be focused on. The sooner you can get your hands on a Bond book (or two or three!) the better. If your child is struggling in a certain area and can't quite master the questions, the Bond books actually suggest you choose the level down and have your child aim to score better to be able to move onto the next level. There is even a progress chart to gauge when to move on and that way your child can aim to do so. It's the same on the website. Check the bibliography at the back of the book for the Amazon link.

Bond books really are a way to save money on tutors, which you may need later on. By working at home on the papers with your child you'll learn the holes in their learning that need repairing. Then, when the time comes for a tutor you'll be able to explain what your child is struggling in. I'm all for tutors, but private tutors can cost quite a bit over time, so it's wise to get them in when you are more informed.

I waited until around six months before exams before I hired her Saturday group math's teacher to come in for one on one session. For me it was about cost. I simply didn't have the funds to do it any earlier. Top private tutors charge anywhere between £40-£65 an hour. I'm not kidding. The reason behind the high charge is because the tutors are usually educated at top universities like Oxford or Cambridge and they know their stuff. A lot of the tutors will have gone through the same exam process so bring personal 11+ experience with them. I think it's quite nice for children to work with a tutor who can share their experience with them, but the cost can put a strain on your purse strings.

Fortunately I am pretty good at English and Comprehension so I didn't need a tutor for her in that area. Plus her teachers at school were excellent so any supplementation at home was a bonus to the learning process and meant she was able to practice to achieve higher marks. Math's on the other hand is not my strength so I knew I would eventually have to fork out for private tuition. If your child is a wiz in Math's then any outside tuition is going to really boost their scores on exam day.

A note on private tuition is to get a tutor on board as soon as you can if you aren't able to help in any key areas. If your son or daughter is in year four then look into group tuition, which is simply a way of spreading cost amongst a very small group. We were only paying £10 per session for group tuition. It was wonderful because she was in a small class of no more than eight on a Saturday morning. There were two teachers in the class so everyone had the opportunity to ask questions. I wish I could tell you it's not necessary to tutor your child, but I can't because private school places are competitive and it's better to have your child prepared than leaving it to chance on the day.

I want to talk a little about Dyslexia and what to do if you suspect that your child may have a form of Dyslexia. My advice is that you know your child better than anyone, and I believe that we as parents who are attuned to our children, will get what I call "a gut feeling" when something isn't right. If you have inkling, no matter how small, then act on it. Find a way to have your child tested as soon as possible. If it is the case that your child has a form of Dyslexia, then you will have proof. This proof will allow you to go to your child's school and request the support of an SEN teacher to help. Furthermore, when you fill out the applications for the secondary schools you can attach it, and that way your child will be given longer time to complete exams. This is really an awesome advantage and that's how I want you to express it to your child. Remind him or her that some of the most famous people are dyslexic. I can give you names, but instead of doing that, simply Google and bring a smile to your child's face and boost their confidence in knowing that they are awesome and just have a different way of processing information, because really that's all it is.

My daughter shared with me how on the day of an 11+ exam, a boy exhaled really loudly and literally got up and pushed his table over. The poor boy just couldn't handle the pressure. Whatever he found difficult caused him to let out his frustration in an aggressive manner. He was escorted out of the room with tears running down his face. When she recounted this story to me I wondered if he had been prepared for the exam or whether nerves just got the better of him. Or whether he had a different undetected learning style? Preparation will help to ease a lot of nerves on exam day and give your child confidence to give every question a go.

Quite a number of top schools are setting the Verbal and Non-Verbal Reasoning tests as a round-one exam to eliminate candidates who would not be able to handle the high academic expectations of their school. It's also a way of filtering out children that have been over-tutored. The exam will usually take place as much as a couple of months before January in year 6. The schools will then invite only the top candidates to come in for the English and Math's exams in January.

The National Foundation for Educational Research (NFER, 2013) states "Non-Verbal Reasoning scores on these tests can indicate a pupil's ability to learn new material in a wide range of school subjects based on their current levels of functioning. These tests have high reliability, typically in the region of 0.90 to 0.95, and good predictive validity, i.e. they are relatively good predictors of future academic attainment."

With regard to the Verbal Reasoning tests, the National Foundation for Educational Research (NFER, 2013) states, "Verbal Reasoning tests consist of a variety of item types, typically including similes, antonyms, analogies, codes and anagrams. Modern verbal reasoning (VR) tests are objective and require a mixture of completion and multiple-choice responses, although some recent versions are entirely in multiple-choice format so that they may be machine-scored via the use of an optically read answer sheet. VR tests are generally designed to provide an overall measure of scholastic ability without having specific curriculum content, principally assessing inferential and deductive skills. The tests have high reliability and are relatively good predictors of subsequent academic attainment."

This is my thought on these exams. Some schools may or may not use them as a round-one exam but your child may find Verbal Reasoning type of questions on the English and Math's exams. I can't stress enough the importance of your child being prepared in this area, so please pick up some resources and start using them as soon as possible.

My daughter earned herself a Bursary place at a highly academic private primary school in Central London. In year 2 and not yet 7 years old, she had to sit an exam of 1 ½ hours, which consisted of, amongst other subjects, Non-Verbal and Verbal Reasoning questions. Luckily, I had the foresight to pick up Bond books designed for her age in this area. It made all the difference and she was offered the place. That was when I realized that with the right preparation children could achieve great things. It comes down to us, the parents, to show them the way.

One of the schools my daughter sat an exam for had every applicant come in for an initial exam of this type. The particular school I am talking about had 700 applicants and after the round-one exam the number went down to 230. The final 230 were then invited to go in and do a residential i.e. sleepover, which is where they assessed her team working skills, physical abilities, as well as the English/Comprehension and Math's. The final number of students that got acceptance letters was eighty children broken down into forty girls and forty boys. Yes, my daughter was one of the girls. I know that had my daughter not been good at the Verbal and Non-Verbal Reasoning then she would not be one of the girls who will be attending a very prestigious boarding school an hour outside of London.

At the particular school I'm talking about, only the students who had achieved well on the residential were invited to audition for the scholarships. It was a big achievement for my daughter to be one of eighty children to gain a place. It also brought to my attention just how coveted places are at top schools. Everyone wants a place but only a small number will be successful. If you follow these steps I know your child will be successful because you will have focused on your goal of Getting Your Child Into a Top School, and that focus will rub off on your child and they will be working toward the same goal with excitement.

Here is something to note: Don't be fooled by the results your child gets in mock exams. I don't believe the results are a true reflection of how your child will do in the entrance exams they take in January of year 6. Firstly, when they take the mock exams they are doing so in their classroom, which is a familiar place. The temperature is set how it always is, and the tables and chairs are ones they know very well. I know I wouldn't be stressed in a familiar environment. Secondly, it is their form teacher that will be handing out the exam and that is comforting unlike someone they don't know. Thirdly, their teacher will also be the one marking the paper and may be biased. Lastly, they will be in the class with all their friends. With all these factors in mind it will be far easier to do well in mock exams, don't you think?

I am not saying the mock exams don't help because they do and I advise you in chapter 9 to go ahead and download past papers for preparation. Bear in mind that the past papers are more of a way of familiarizing your child with the type of questions they might see on an entrance exam. New exams are written every year and some say they are getting harder each year due to the fact a lot of parents are over-tutoring their child solely based on past papers. Balance is the key to preparation.

I want to talk about the creative writing process and how you should go about helping your child develop their writing skills. This is what I did. I started off by asking my daughter to tell me about the stories she was reading. I asked for details about the characters and where the story took place. Was it in the past, present day or future. I wanted her to share as much as she could. Then I would question her by asking things like "what would you have done differently if you were that character?" At first she would say something like "I dunno". She was wondering where I was going with all this so I played a little psychology on her. I got into the characters and said "if that were me I would have done so and so". I'd make it funny to get her into it. Kids have great imaginations naturally. You can make any child get into their imagination simply by allowing yourself the freedom to do the same.

What I was doing was pushing her to use her own imagination to create different endings to her favorite stories. That's basically what the creative writing part of the exam paper is all about. There is the technical side of course, which comprises of the beginning, which sets up the story; the middle, which houses all the action; and the end, which ties it all together. They'll need to develop their skills of creating a running thread throughout the story, but honestly they will get there because they will be learning it in class. Any help you can give at home is only going to add to their confidence.

There are resources online and in bookstores that will be able to help with developing creative writing skills. Some guides will start the story and have the child complete it using their own imagination. Other guides will give you a name of a character and the time the story takes place and that's all, leaving the rest of the creative process to your child. I think both are good exercises. You never know how this part of the exam will be laid out. Knowing how to write a good piece of creative writing is important so the focus must be on the ability to write a very good beginning, a middle where the characters have really come to life; and an end that pulls it all together and will grab the attention of the examiner.

If your child really struggles in this area then why not make it fun at home by asking your child to create an illustration to go along with their story? You don't have to be a Picasso to enjoy drawing, so please encourage him or her to do so. If they really don't like drawing then encourage them to build something or make something out of Fimo, polymer clay that can be baked in the oven to harden. Children really enjoy using their hands to create tiny figurines they can use in play so this is a good way of sparking their imagination. If they can see the characters then they can write about them.

There are loads of websites and apps that you can go to or download that will enhance the learning process. The BBC has a kids website where they can go to, to discover and learn interesting facts on subjects they are learning in school. For example take the subject History, you can go to **http://www.bbc.co.uk/history/forkids** and you'll find that they have designed interactive history games. For the Egyptians they have a game called Mummy Maker, which is filled with information about how the deceased were embalmed. My daughter loves using this free resource. I suggest you have a browse and enjoy it with your child.

Don't forget to go to the app store and browse the educational games they have for children. There are so many apps that I don't know where to start but just go and have a look to see what takes your child's fancy. Quite often the apps are free and you can download them on your child's Ipad or mobile phone and at the very least, the family computer. When you say to your child "please go to the computer and play that math quiz game for twenty minutes sweetheart" watch their face light up because any opportunity to go online is fun for kids, even when it's educational. The games are supplementation to the practice test papers, and a way to let off some steam whilst still learning. Not bad eh?

My point in this is that I want your child's journey to be as enjoyable as possible because just like love, fun also builds confidence. If you can make the learning process fun, then you will be instilling a love of learning in your child that will go on well after they take the entrance exams.

All the focus on the academic side might create a classroom of competition. Your child may be feeling like he or she isn't good enough if a classmate scores higher on in-class exams. Some children may get jealous if your child starts doing better than they are. My daughter experienced both scenarios. Luckily she loves to talk at bedtime and tell me about her day. It was at those quiet times where I found out how she was really feeling. When I realized what was going on I came up with the right words to make her feel better. Maybe you might need to use these words or something similar: "Honey this is not a competition. I want you to just strive to be the best you because that's all you can do. Be happy when your friends do well and pleased for yourself when you do well too. If a friend feels down then show them kindness and if you feel down, either talk to a friend for support or talk to me. Me and your dad are here for you and we love you no matter what". Of course she wanted to do well and was disappointed when things didn't go her way, but the support gave her the security to try her best. Remember that a child that has the support of his or her parents can face any situation head on. A prepared child will look forward to taking their exams because they know they are ready and will be aiming to do their best.

STEP 5: ASSESSING SCHOOLS

"Be independent of the good opinion of other people." - Abraham Maslow

Assessing schools is when it starts to become real to both you and your child. It's the flicker of light at the end of the tunnel. By visiting the schools it's the boost your child will need to reach the goal. The moment my daughter and I started visiting schools I noticed a change in her attitude. She began to behave a little older. I think she could see that going to secondary school was the beginning of something great in her life.

There is so much information online about schools. On some popular websites you can read an amazing parent review about a school, then a horrible review about the same school will follow. It can do your head in. Whose opinion do you trust? How many times have you read a bad review about something and then you find yourself researching to see if there is any more negative information out there on the subject? I know I've done that many times and it wasn't until I stopped did I realize that that was the wrong way to go about research. It was backwards. I say look for honest reviews first from individuals to determine whether or not you want to know more.

When I wanted to know about a school I went online and looked to see if they had a recent Ofsted report I could read. Here is the link **http://reports.ofsted.gov.uk/** and for Independent schools there is the Independent Schools Inspectorate **http://www.isi.net/reports/**. Please start here first, and after you've checked out these links then have a look for other reviews so you can weigh it all up.

The first step in selecting schools isn't that difficult because secondary schools will have dedicated open days that allow you and your child to be taken on a tour of the school. Children in different year groups will greet you and take you on a walk-around of the school, showing you classrooms and the sports facilities. They'll ask your son or daughter what they are into and ask if they want to head there first. This will make your child feel connected to the tour guide and might even have them talking. You'll probably be impressed with how well the children speak. Not every child will take part in touring prospective students around. I think they choose the most outgoing children to make a good impression. I don't blame the schools. I mean would you really want a very quiet child taking you around. Remember, private school is big business so they need to make sure they make a good impression on your child and you.

But don't get distracted by the bright child speaking highly of the school. I saw a lot of parents walking around with their heads up in the clouds. I don't know if they were reminiscing about their own childhood or what was going on back at the office. I on the other hand took the chance to peek at all the nooks and crannies as I entered classrooms. I also wanted to see what they had to offer. Like, if good nutrition is your thing then pay attention to what's going on in the dining room. We visited one of the top, highly academic schools in London and I was surprised to see a vending machine with chocolate bars and crisps. I have a problem with children filling up on unhealthy snacks so that was a red flag for me.

If your child has special educational needs then make sure you enquire if they have a SEN team that handles the educational needs that your child has. Also, when you look at the Ofsted report, check the number of SEN students. If the number is low then that may be an indication that they don't have the staff to help. Trust me when a school has staff to handle Special Educational Needs that information spreads throughout parenting websites. Word of mouth is a good thing in this instance because without it how would you know that the school would meet your son or daughter's needs. It always comes down to how much information you can get your hands on when choosing a school and that's the point of this book. I want to inform you to empower you so you can choose the school that is right for your child.

I'm big on grounds where the child can do all their sports on campus. Because my daughter went to a small primary school with the name of the school having the word 'house' in, it meant that it was actually in an old Georgian Home and it didn't have a playground. They have to use the park for outside activities. It sounds really nice and it is on the one hand because the children were out in nature on sunny days, but if the weather was really rainy or snowy they didn't get to go outside for breaks to let off some steam. As you can imagine, living in London that was quite often. I knew I wanted her secondary school to have an indoor gym as well as an on-campus outdoor space. Your child will be at their secondary school for a minimum of five years and a further two if they stay through their A-levels, which takes it up to seven years. Think about whether or not you could see your son or daughter being happy for that long at a particular school.

If your schedule doesn't allow you to go to an Open Day then not to worry because it's not the only time you can visit a school. You can contact a school and ask for a private visit. I'm all for them because I think a private visit will give you a better picture of what's going on during school life. You will be able to get a truer feel of the energy in classrooms. When a teacher is informed that a parent will be visiting they will put on a great performance, but teens are not going to smile brightly just because the teacher wants them too, in fact they'll do the opposite. If they are bored during a lesson, because the teacher is not engaging, then it will be written all over their faces and in their body language. When I visited primary schools the children were all sweet and cheery but at secondary schools it's a whole different kettle of fish. That's fine by me because I want to see for myself, without the fanfare how children are in the classrooms.

You'll want to pay attention to what the energy of the teachers is like. My personal opinion is that if a teacher stays in a job too long, then you no longer get the best from them. Going to work becomes habitual and so does ones teaching style. Find out how long they've taught at the school. You want to pay attention to how they answer your questions. Antenna's up please.

I'd be asking questions like, "what new technology are you using to teach your students?" Students today are different to students ten years ago. In 2014 the BBC stated that seventy percent of UK schools are using tablets to engage and teach children. When you are paying top buck for your child's education then I believe the schools need to make sure they have the latest teaching equipment, computers and tablets in the classroom. If state schools are using tablets in the class then so should fee-paying and grammar schools. The world is constantly evolving technologically, and with smart phones children need facilities that grab their attention. This is why you'll notice a lot of academies and free schools opening up around London because the educational leaders know that the way today's children are taught needs to come from a modern-forward- thinking perspective. So, make sure you ask the right questions on Open Days. Please don't feel you have to rush through the tour even if the person touring you appears to be in a rush. You control the pace so you can ask questions and get them answered. Remember this is your son or daughters academic future so go for it. As stated before you can always come back for a second or third visit. If you are choosing a fee-paying school, then remember the fees are not cheap and you don't want to find yourself pulling your child out because you didn't do your due diligence. If you pull your child out without a terms notice then you have to pay the next terms fees. Imagine just giving away 5-7k. That can't be a good feeling especially if all you had to do was ask questions in the beginning. When it comes to grammar schools and top state schools, you still need to ask as many questions as possible. Although you won't be losing money you will lose time and may find your son or daughter without a school place if you pull them out. I've sat with my clients and helped them to find alternative schools if they found they have made the wrong decision about a school. I usually suggest the parents meet with the form teacher or the head teacher to discuss any issues and if they cannot get them resolved then wait until they have found a solution like a better suited school for their child, before withdrawing him or her. It's just common sense really, but when it comes to our children, that can fly out the window right? I believe if we can control our emotions then we can make better decisions.

Just as I had my list of things I wanted for my daughter at secondary school, I also know her well enough to know that she needed a facility that catered to her out –of- class likes. My daughter loves Art and Design so I looked at schools that were also big on Art and Design. She also loves swimming so schools that had their own swimming pool was also high on the list. Education is not the only thing that matters to children. To be honest, they just want to be happy and to find a way to have fun at school. Striking the balance is crucial.

As parents, we need to make sure we are not trying to redesign our childhoods through our children. Our aim in getting our children into a top school should be because we know it's the best for them, and will give them greater opportunities in the future, not because we feel like it's something we should have had. How many times have you heard people say "I always wanted to play piano, so I'm going to make sure my child plays" Whose dream is that? We all do it, so, don't guilt trip yourself. I'm just calling it out so you are aware that even selecting a school can be about us and not our child and it needs to be in reverse.

There were quite a few parents I met along the private school journey that applied for highly academic schools when what their children really wanted to do was perform on stage. Some of these children were really good at drama too and not that good academically. But for whatever reason these parents just didn't take their children's personality into consideration. They were fearful that their child wouldn't amount to anything if they went into the arts. Kind of sad but I've had conversations with individuals who thought like that. Come to think of it, I was one of those people. The irony is that I spent over twenty years in the music industry as a singer. I traveled to places like Russia, Greece, France, Germany, Italy, and even learned I was pregnant whilst on tour with my band in Istanbul Turkey. I think I turned out fine. Okay, so I have a few tattoos and pictures of my hair dyed blue, but I had a great time and a thousand experiences that I wouldn't trade in. Not to forget the many people I met that were touched by my music. I also learned a load of transferable skills that I would never have gained working in an office. As a result, I can speak in front of a room of thousands and feel completely at ease. I know what equipment is needed for presentations and I can easily manage a group of people because I fronted bands and understand the benefit of good communication skills. This is just a few of the transferable skills I've learned from being in the music industry.

Unfortunately a lot of people are more concerned with keeping up with the Jones's, worried about what others will think if they choose to apply to schools that are really sporty or artsy. I mean seriously, should you care? Once I questioned my own actions, choosing schools with my daughter became so much more about her. Those that place their faith in other people's opinion of schools often make the wrong decision. In the end, they are disappointed and stressed after opening the post box to more than one rejection letter and their child is left without a school to attend in September. This DOES happen and I know many people it's happened to. They are left begging the Registrars to give their child a place, only to be told that the best they can do is put him or her on the waiting list, which is usually so long that you can forget about it. I will say that it does help to have a consultant on board to make a phone call for you if you find yourself in that situation.

A competitive parent with an agenda based entirely on their own desire and not that of their child, may react to a school rejection letter in such a way that could be, should I say, embarrassing. When my daughter sat her 11+ exams one of her classmates didn't get a call for an interview, which meant that she would not be getting an offer. The mother was so sure that they made a mistake that she phoned the school to question their decision. When she retold the story she recounted how she actually gave them a piece of her mind. I thought that isn't what we need to be doing as parents.

Needless to say they didn't budge on their decision. In the end the child accepted a place at a school that actually suited her artistic abilities. I imagine that the child will be much happier.

Assessing schools should be done without concern about what other parents feel about your family's school selection. It's no one's business but your own. They aren't going to be paying the fees for you or driving your child to school, and even if they did, it's not about what they want anyway. I'm saying this because my experience was filled with other moms speaking loudly for or against my choices and the funny thing is that these same mothers had never stepped on campus at the secondary schools they shared their weak opinions of. It was all hearsay and quite often based on some incident that happened years prior but had spread like Chinese Whispers in a playground, completely diluted of any facts. Do your due diligence, the same due diligence you would put in when buying a house.

When visiting schools quite a number of parents are thinking more about the first year of secondary school. They also tend to be primarily concerned about whether any of the school leavers are going to Oxford or Cambridge. If the parents aren't from the UK then they are usually only familiar with these two names and expect their child to be able to go there if they attend the school they are visiting. You have to understand a major point and that is that Oxford and Cambridge are the top in the country, are highly competitive and may not be the right university of choice for your child in the future. And that's ok.

Another thing parents make the mistake in doing is that they assume that there must be good careers counselors on board because it's a private or grammar school. I'd argue that they probably didn't even think that far ahead. My daughter's father tried to shush me when I started to talk about the future, when our daughter would be in sixth form, and questioned a teacher on what their school had in place in terms of preparation for university interviews and personal statement writing. I was thinking about all of these things because if I didn't I would be the one to feel really bad if her secondary school choice didn't have good teams in place to prepare her for her future.

Have you ever heard of The Russell Group of Universities? They are a group of the top universities that have received the highest mark of excellence in the UK and are recognized throughout the world as top research and learning institutions. When researching schools you'll usually find information about where the A-level students got university places. If you see any of these schools on the list then it's a very good indication that the school knows how to prepare their students. There are 24 Universities that have received this mark and they are as follows:

- University of Birmingham
- University of Bristol
- University of Cambridge
- Cardiff University
- Durham University
- University of Edinburgh
- University of Exeter
- University of Glasgow
- Imperial College London
- King's College London
- University of Leeds
- University of Liverpool
- London School of Economics & Political Science
- University of Manchester
- Newcastle University
- University of Nottingham
- University of Oxford
- Queen Mary University of London
- Queen's University Belfast
- University of Sheffield
- University of Southampton
- University College London
- University of Warwick
- University of York

I had no clue about what the Russell Group of universities were until I started visiting schools when my daughter was in year 4. During a Head Mistress's speech she spoke about how wonderful her school was and how well her students did in A-levels. She followed that with a mention about her students going off to study at the Russell Group universities when they left. I thought it sounded like some underground cult for the exclusive, so the moment I got on the train I did a search on my smart-phone. Sure enough the universities under the Russell Group banner, are the cream of the crop of universities. In the list you'll notice Oxford and Cambridge are not the only top universities in the UK. Maybe you knew that already, but because I'm an outsider I didn't. I have to tell you that I'm so glad I found this information out because it gave me more confidence. When we did our walk around during open day at secondary schools, I was able to ask the right questions and not have starry eye syndrome. In America local schools and a lot of private schools aren't so grand like the schools in the UK. So it's really easy to be impressed and forget to ask key questions.

So how many applications do top schools receive is the question I wanted answers to and I'm sure you want to know as well. So, I contacted a few of the top secondary schools in London to see how many applications they had received for very few places on offer. One private school in West London had received 1100 applications (up by 300 from the previous years) and get this, they only offer 120 places which means that only 11% out of 1100 applicants were successful and 980 children weren't. Why had so many people applied to a school where the odds weren't very good? Could it be they read that the school sent 30 of their students to Oxbridge in 2013? It is pretty incredible. I spoke to some mums and they said that they knew their child wasn't working at the top of the class in their primary school but they had applied hoping that on the day their child would score high enough to earn a place. Some of these mother's hadn't even considered tutoring and hadn't even heard of Bond papers before I mentioned it.

I phoned a top girls school in Central London to ask how many applicants they had received and I was informed that they had an additional four hundred applicants this year (January 2015). I asked what she thought was going on and she said that parents are so worried about not getting a place for their child that they are willing to apply to as many schools as possible. I have a friend who actually did just that and shelled out application fees for eleven schools. It did pay off because their daughter got three offers. Some it worked for and others it was a fail. I know that seems incredible but that's the truth. Your child still needs to be prepared for these exams. My thoughts on this is that if you can afford to shell out £1500 for application fees, then go for it but choose schools that suit your child. I advise my clients to do the same thing because at the end of the day I want you to get your child into a top school and if it happens to be a private school then do what it takes to make it a possibility.

You are still going to have to assess secondary schools and do as much research as you possibly can. Don't be afraid to visit schools more than once or twice. Each time you go to an Open Day or for a private visit, your eyes will be opened wider than before. Because my daughter and I visited the same schools more than once or twice, we found it easy to write down our short list. I felt confident that the names of the schools I wrote down suited her personality and she made sure the schools had the kind of extracurricular activities she liked combined with strong academics. Now all we had to do was take that list and narrow it down to our top choices. This leads us to the next step. Before we move on, if this is all a bit overwhelming please contact me for a one off consultation session where I can help ease the pressure. Contact me by email at **goodmumsguide@gmail.com** and I'll be glad to help either by Skype call or in person if you are in London.

STEP 6: SCHOOL SELECTION YEAR 5 AND TUTORS

"When kids made a decision for themselves they have a vested interest in showing they were right. Lee wanted to prove to me that he had made the right choice so he worked hard and did well. If we'd forced him to go to college somewhere else all the incentives would've been different. Then he would have had a motive to prove that we were wrong."
- Cokie Roberts, From This Day Forward

So, here you find yourself looking at your lovely son or daughter who is fast approaching their exams, and although it's exciting it's also a bit emotional. Emotional, because you know, that in the not so distant future, he or she will be entering Secondary school or in our case heading off to boarding school. I've shed a lot of tears mostly because I'm a soppy so in so. I've done so in the privacy of my bathroom because the last thing I need is my daughter to be concerned with my psychological babble. I want her to go out into the new era in her life with all my love and support.

You are getting closer to the finish line, and the buzz is undoubtedly in the air amongst other mums. Some mums will be holding their cards close to their chest. These chest players are simply fearful of your child getting a place that they feel their child deserves. These individuals have fear written all over their faces. When you ask them where they are applying they'll respond with something like "we're still not sure", unable to look you in the eyes, and all the while they have sent their applications in six months prior to your conversation. I have to laugh when I look back at those times. I knew what was on the line, which was big for all of us, so I get the card holding. We wanted our child to get one of those coveted places; places that were limited to very small numbers. Yes it gets weird when selections are being made but that's how it is. The trick is that you just need to be aware of it and not get caught up in the drama.

The head teacher of a small school may have you come in to discuss your choices individually, or may call a group meeting for all parents to come in and listen to advice on schools they consider to be good choices for their students. It's a perfect time to ask for advice on what they feel would suit your child. Don't forget they are with your child five days a week so they know how your child behaves academically and socially. I think its fair to say that your child's teacher probably has a pretty good idea on what they are talking about. There are some teachers who are blatantly scared to make suggestions. It may seem strange to you, but understand this, the reason is that they know the competition is great so if they make a suggestion and you take it but your child doesn't get an offer from those particular schools then they are to blame. I know of one mother who was told that she should consider applying to a theatre school because her daughter was not strong academically. Number one, that's an insult to suggest that theatre schools aren't academic. Secondly, and most importantly, her mother knew full well that her daughter never expressed any love for acting on stage. I just shook my head. The teacher in question was so full of fear of her reputation being tainted in any way that she shelled out advice that wasn't advice at all. The particular teacher I'm talking about actually said to my child "sometimes I think you're really stupid". Imagine how great I felt when my daughter got three acceptance letters and two scholarships from top secondary schools. You are probably wondering how I handled that situation, well I spoke to my ex-husband and had him go in and speak with the teacher- who happened to be the head teacher. I did this because I didn't want to lose my cool. My daughter was on a bursary and I didn't want to jeopardize her situation at the school. Sometimes one has to make decisions that will strengthen ones position. I was not about to teach my child to exit a situation because it's uncomfortable. If I had done that then that would be a pattern in her life. No, her father handled it diplomatically and we lifted my daughter's spirits by teaching her to be strong and always smile even at your enemy. That wasn't very nice to say to a child, and as you can imagine I wasn't very happy, so you can see why from personal experience that even your child's teacher may not have an in-depth clue about who your child is. If you find that this is the case, then my advice is don't even go to the meeting. But if you do go, go to simply grab any tidbits that can be useful. At the end of the day, choosing a school for your child should be done based on proper assessment and suitability for your child and that's it. But it is up to you to make the final decision, because at the end of the day you know your child better than anyone. Just be open-minded.

After the final selection, start printing past exam papers from the schools' websites. This is really important because your child will feel connected to the different schools and will be more interested in doing well in his or her exams. It makes such a huge difference to the child's preparation when they have a picture of what they are aiming for. My daughter got so excited about the possibility of attending one of the schools we chose that she began to work harder toward her dreams. She knew where she was headed if she put in the time to get high marks on her entrance exams. She did really well too and as mentioned she got offers from all three of the schools we applied to. Plus she got two art scholarships and although she wasn't successful in the music scholarship she auditioned for, the mere fact that she put her best foot forward gave her an incredible sense of self and that was worth the effort of going for it.

I subscribe to the thought that "faith without actions is dead". In other words, you can believe that your child should go to a school because they are awesome, but if you don't prepare (that's the action) then you will not have the success you want. Parents please remember that hard work and commitment from you and not just your child, is crucial in achieving success. They are just youngsters who need guidance and assurance from us to get where they want to go in life and this is a wonderful opportunity for you to help get them on the right path toward success. The bonus is the discipline gained will be valuable, as they become young adults.

We are only three short months away from our daughter stepping onto her school campus (at the time of writing this). She will be boarding away from home for three weeks at a time and I can't tell you how excited she is. She recently took her final year 6 exams and has scored 100 marks in spelling and the high 90's in English. And after taking a Math's exam, results show that she is working at level 6, which is what level 13 year olds work at! Her confidence is so high that she hasn't had to over study for anything at all, simply because she now believes in what she is capable of and is walking in that knowing. I attribute this to the effort that we put in together during the preparation for exams. I am one proud momma and I want you to feel the same way, so please, if you only take away one piece of information from this book let it be that preparation really is the key to success.

To tutor or not to tutor is the question. My answer to this is yes. I believe you should tutor if there are holes in your child's learning. I want your child to be confident that they can give every question at the very least an educated guess. It would be sad to imagine your child unable to even try to answer a question on their entrance exams. Tutoring can give your child a better chance in achieving success. A lot of secondary schools are getting hip to the fact that children are being 'over-tutored'. We the parents don't really understand what over-tutoring is all about and some decide to not tutor as a result. It was really confusing to others and me, so I did a bit of research to discover what was actually meant by 'over-tutoring'. I contacted five schools and with a nice hello I was able to talk with three school registrars and all three gave me the same answer. 'Over-tutoring' is when say, you have a child who is an average student and you decide to tutor them five days a week. The tutoring will teach them how to answer the questions and will even make it possible for them to get into a really academic school. The problem appears when the child is in year 7 and is struggling to keep up with the pressure of the academic workload designed for students that are quite gifted academically. Based on the entrance exam results the child should not being having such difficulties. Teachers began to see patterns of this happening to a high enough percentage of students to the point where a red flag had to go up. It became clear to the head teachers, after speaking with the students and parents, that they had been tutored daily in preparation for the entrance exam. They decided that something had to be done to cull out students that didn't have what it naturally took to come to their school. This is one of the reasons that more top schools are doing the Verbal and Non-Verbal Reasoning tests. As I mentioned earlier, a top school is built on reputation so to have a high number of children not doing well will bring them down the league tables.

I recently had the opportunity to sit in on a head teachers meeting in Wandsworth. One head told me how she is under a lot of pressure from parents who want their child to get into a top school. She stated that in the past couple of years she has had year 5 and 6 children crying because they feel the pressure from their parents to perform well to get into schools like St. Paul's for example. I think we as parents have felt the peer pressure to get our children to the best schools possible and if we don't then there is the feeling that we've failed as parents. I say 'we' because at a certain point I believed the same thing. But as I mentioned earlier it is imperative that we look at schools that suit our child, the individual, and forget about keeping up with the Kardashians'. I cannot stress enough how your child should not be put under pressure to the point of causing them anxiety. I've done it and shared that information and I'm not proud of it. If you find that you are putting pressure on your child, pull back and take it easy. It's not worth your child hating you. Tutoring is not about getting YOU into a top school. This is about helping your child be the best he or she can be.

Now, if you have discovered holes in your child's learning, then I would suggest tutoring one to two days a weeks max. A good tutor will leave your child with homework to complete during the week. You should make sure you are aware of what the homework is and be near to give a hand if it's needed. Remember, you are going to be mucking in as much as possible.

The reward is great and you should be seeing the fruit of you and your child's labor in classroom results and the great attitude your child has because he or she knows mom is on board. Children want their parents' support, so give it freely.

When you have a tutor coming to your home try not to get involved. This may be difficult for some of you but it's important. During these times you should be a silent partner. Don't start offering food and drinks. The tutor is only with your son or daughter for an hour; so let it be spent without unnecessary conversation. At the end of the session you should feel free to ask any brief questions regarding your child's progress. Keep it short and sweet because a good tutor usually has a list of clients to get to.

If you have chosen a tutor and you can see that your child just doesn't gel with him or her then first speak to your darling daughter or son and see what the problem is. I want you to avoid bouncing from one tutor to the next without proper cause. You might find that your young darling simply isn't into being tutored and it's nothing to do with a personality clash. If this is the case then remind them of the goal to get into a top school. When my daughter felt a bit bored with it all, I would make it a point to periodically go to the websites of the three schools we had chosen to remind her of how awesome the schools were and why she was working so hard. It really helped. We would lie in bed and talk about what the school had to offer. My daughter would let her imagination wander and she'd ask questions about the facilities, wondering out-loud what the teachers would be like. She'd recount to me the many students she met during the open days. It would be the boost that she needed and the next time her tutor came she would be way more receptive to the session. Long-term goals can seem, well, a long way off to children, so a reminder of what they are trying to achieve is a very good idea. It will also help you carry on as well.

If you find your child still doesn't click with the tutor then by all means terminate the relationship, but first find a new one before sacking the one you have because a good tutor is hard to find as they are in high demand. If you discover that the wait for the tutor you want is a few weeks away, unless your original tutor is a real meanie, then please tell your child they are going to have to grin and bear it for a while longer. Life doesn't always deliver to us what we want, when we want it and it is good to learn this as a child because it is what it is.

The summer before year 6 is crucial because it's the lead up to the final term before exams. I suggest you use the six weeks to continue with preparing your child. Of course no child wants to do math or creative writing over the summer unless they are a genius. Most children are not geniuses and find watching cartoons and playing on their Ipad way more fun than school stuff. You might find that you are going to have to be really creative with the learning process during the summer. If you are a full time parent then get online and find out what your city has to offer that is both educational and fun. At the very least, if you choose just fun for your activities then the next day set an assignment where your child has to write two pages about their day out. At the age of ten they should be able to do this. You might have to make suggestions but not so much that you are writing the paper. Encourage your child to get excited to share about their day out.

Step 7: Applications for Entry, Scholarships and Bursaries

"Recognize the gift that is your child. Everything else is a bonus."
- KK Harris

You have assessed the schools and have made your final decisions which schools to apply to and are now ready to fill in the applications. You are probably also considering Scholarships and want to know about Bursaries. This is what you've been reading me talk about so it's time for me to give you explanations that will help you to determine what these might mean for you. Firstly, applications are self- explanatory. You download the application from the school and fill out the information. Just make sure you answer all the questions and include your email address and phone number. It sounds straightforward I know, but when you have more than a few of these applications it can feel a bit overwhelming and you might find yourself rushed and leave things out and that's the last thing you want to do. So make sure you go over your completed application before sending it in. Even ask your partner or friend to look it over in case you've left anything out. If the school you are applying is a grammar or church school then you'll have to apply to the borough as well as fill out the schools application. This is very important and if you get it wrong then you can easily blow an opportunity for your child.

Scholarship applications as mentioned are all about excellence and you'll find you are required to attach references from your child's private instructors or coaches to support the application. If your child is auditioning for a music scholarship you will have to attach their Grade ABRSM certificates. If your child has not achieved the minimum Grade on their first and second instruments required by the schools you are applying to, then please don't apply because you'll only be wasting time. There are a lot of children that have achieved what they are looking for and priority is given to them.

Sports scholarships also require references and try-outs, which will require your child to come in and spend an afternoon playing a variety of sports. If your child's talents lie in a specific sport then it is likely the focus will be on that sport. It is entirely up to the school, so find out what their try-outs entail. Try to get well informed as far in advance as possible before

55

the try-outs. As I mentioned earlier, I failed to be fully informed about the music scholarship requirements, which caused unnecessary stress for my daughter and me. Please learn from my mistakes.

Art scholarships usually require a technical drawing skills session so please make sure your child has worked on honing those skills. We set aside time for her to work on her technical drawing skills to make sure she was really prepared on the days of the scholarship session.

Another thing the art departments will be looking for is how a child might set a scene by having them bring in objects from home to arrange and draw. A further option could be that a brief will be given to applicants over the Christmas period and the children will have to create several or more pieces using mixed media working toward a final piece. All of the above mentioned is what my daughter experienced. We were all very shocked at how much she had to do. They are only ten and eleven years old for goodness sake, yet it seemed like they were teenagers doing A-levels. It was all a bit much. In hindsight it really taught my daughter how to plan a project under a certain amount of time and deliver to a high standard. It was nice to receive two art scholarship offers, which were worth 2k off the school fees annually.

Drama and Dance will both require auditions. Children will be asked to prepare a monologue and should be prepared to act out a piece of acting with staff or other children. This is left up to the school. Any certifications or previous acting experience as in theatre performances outside of school should be noted. If your child has an agent this should also be attached and can be used as a reference as well as one from their tutors.

Remember Scholarships are all about prestige and excellence. The lucky children will be representing the school. With scholarships comes great responsibility, so please be aware that if your child is fortunate, they will be required to focus much of their free time to attend additional classes in their specialist area. They will also be expected to perform for special events and performances. The top athletes will also be supported and encouraged to work hard to represent the school in matches. They will get special treatment and guidance by the coaches and they will need you to understand when they are simply too exhausted to help out around the house because they want to sleep. The rewards are great for both you and them. If they can keep pace, then those with scholarships usually have great university opportunities such as getting scholarships to study abroad in America. My youngest sister was fortunate to get an Academic and Sports Scholarship to a private university, which meant her education was entirely free. Wouldn't that be a load off your shoulders? I have met quite a number of young English students who have also been lucky to gain scholarships to go to university in America and the opportunity quite literally changed their lives and opened the door to further opportunities when they returned to the UK.

Bursary applications should be submitted on time because a missed deadline can blow your vision of a wonderful secondary education for your child. Of course this applies to private schools so if you aren't going that route then don't worry. If you are, then please don't delay.

Be honest and transparent when filling out the bursary application. I've read stories in the newspapers of families trying to hide the fact that they have a second property only to be found out by a simple Land Registry check. When they get found out they are red flagged as not to be trusted. Needless to say the child never gets an offer. It's so unfair when people behave like this because if they were just honest they would have probably found that they were eligible for a percentage off the school fees. The idea is that if you hold a second property then you should re-mortgage to pay for your child's education. It really does make sense to invest in your son or daughter's education if it's a private education you want.

Lets face it, private school fees are exorbitant and at a minimum are around 15k a year, which is a wage for a lot of people. Schools have specialists to look over applications and take the income and expenses into account to determine how much of a bursary award they can offer a family. They also know how much they can afford to give away in terms of free places to children who wouldn't be able to afford to go to their school if they didn't receive a bursary. So it is only right to be honest because if you aren't you will be taking away a child's opportunity to flourish.

I had an interesting conversation with an independent financial assessor I know regarding what the school will look at when determining which child will receive a bursary award. He told me that each school has their own set of criteria. One of the schools he was contracted for looked for applications where the family had shown an ability to make a financial contribution toward school fees. By offering part bursary places to families it enabled the school to give a larger amount of children a top education. If private education is what you are after and are able to contribute 25%-50% of the fees then your child would more than likely be one that gets a bursary place dependent on how well he or she does on the entrance exam plus interview.

But where does that leave bright students whose families in no way can afford a private education but really feels their child would thrive in a private school for personal reasons? My suggestion is that you contact the schools you want to apply and find out as much information as you can when it comes to how they make their decisions on bursary places. Some will be open about it whereas other schools will keep it entirely confidential and it's their prerogative to do so. Another suggestion is that you need to make sure that the schools you apply offer more than just a few bursary places.

Another note, gone are the days where a single mother would automatically get a bursary for her child just because she was on benefits or very low wages. I recently tweeted that "there are 2 million single parent homes in the UK, we are not alone." Times have truly changed and private schools are aware of this, so when they are handing out bursary places, a hard luck story is not going to pull on their heartstrings honey. It's your ability to contribute. Saying that, there are schools in the country that are giving bright children a top education due to the kindness of past alumni and philanthropists long since gone, which have left great sums of money to make sure these bright children reach their full potential. My daughter will be attending one such school.

These schools that give more than just a few bursaries are very selective and they are just as tough to get into as some very top secondary schools, because of how great the competition is and how incredibly tough the exams and interview processes are.

If you are divorced or legally separated then make sure you have your documents to prove it because you will be asked when it comes to bursary places. If you have lost the documents get them together after reading this so you are ready to go.

At the end of the day this little book is all about preparation. I wrote it so you would be clear on what is required in all areas. I know there's a lot to do but you and your young one are nearing the finish line. I'm so excited for you!

If you are not in the country and would like for me to be your consultant and help guide you through the above process then please don't hesitate to get in contact with me via email at **goodmumsguide@gmail.com**

Step 8: Interview Techniques

"We tell our children not to speak to strangers, so how do we expect them to handle an interview with a stranger/head teacher of a school? You help them create something that they are proud of and happy to talk about."
- KK Harris

For some children the idea of sitting with a stranger and answering questions, particularly with a teacher they don't know, will be daunting. For others it will be a walk in the park. Remember how you've felt every time you had a job interview, that anxious feeling in your stomach. Or how about that jittery feeling you get before doing a presentation? Now imagine being ten or eleven years old and how it must feel. Your child may have feelings of being judged or not liked. These are all feelings of fear. Remember fear isn't real so you can help your child get over these negative feelings. It just takes a bit of effort on your part.

It's easy for us to tell our children to go in there and let there light shine. I say that to my daughter all the time, but it wasn't until it was time for exams that I realized she was quite nervous about the whole thing. She didn't want to disappoint me and the result was a shedding of tears one night when we were practicing for the interviews. She told me that she was worried that she was going to say something wrong. When I heard her cry for reassurance I answered the call. I started off reminding her that she is awesome and should try to relax. That wasn't enough, so I said, " I know! We are going to do an interview project!" Ty's form teacher had told her and her classmates that they should bring something they could talk about to their interviews like a photo album. It's the 21st Century and a photo album is not going to cut it. I wanted my daughter to stand out in the crowd. Like I mentioned there are upwards of 1100 applicants for school places, and at some private schools interviews take place before exams. Imagine interviewing all those children, there has to be something distinguishable in order for one to be remembered. So that's what we went for.

At the time my daughter was really into sculpting figurines out of Fimo. So we came up with the idea that she should sculpt over a dozen birds, of different breeds from different countries. We decided to call the project

'Crowded Spaces' which represented London, a culturally diverse city. My daughter's primary school is in the West End and she found it super crowded with all the shoppers marching by and bumping into her on Oxford Street.

The project took a good six weeks to finish because she was so busy. I went to a local store on Portobello Road and bought a gorgeous birds cage for £10 and she decorated the cage with artificial flowers we picked up from Poundland. We went out to our local park and collected little branches for the birds to sit on in the cage. She also sculpted a bowl in her Sunday art class and placed it inside the cage for a birdbath. She sculpted a Heron, Finches, a Swan, a mommy and baby Owl, Parakeets and a host of other birds. Some hung in the cage with fishing line appearing to be flying, while an owl sat in a corner of the cage as if longing to be free. It was a lovely project, which allowed her to escape into her imagination. I have to say I was impressed. While she put together the project it was the perfect opportunity to ask her mock interview questions. It made the process an enjoyable experience for her.

I would suggest you have your child do a project to take to their interview. It will give your child the confidence they need. Children love creating something with their own hands. It doesn't matter that your child isn't a master artist. If you put in the time to look up ideas online for inspiration, then you will find that there will be something that will spark your child's interest. The project doesn't need to cost an arm and a leg. As mentioned we didn't spend much at all for supplies. I think the total was around £15-£20. I think that's worth the confidence your child will gain. Most importantly it will obliterate all fear and give your child an edge on the competition. At one school the Head Teacher said "No one has ever brought me in something so special." Apparently, most of the fifteen-minute interview was spent discussing her project. When my daughter came out of every one of her interviews she was always smiling and that made me feel so good.

The project can be done over an extended period of time giving a break from the test papers. All you have to do is come up with something fun with your child. Whatever it is that your child likes to do can be used as inspiration. Even a favorite cartoon can be turned into a project with something as simple as a cardboard box, bottle tops, string, glue and images you can download off the Internet. So go for it!

Another tip for the interview is that you should have your child brush up on a bit of history, as well as general knowledge. My daughter was showed a picture of a historical figure and asked if she knew who it was. Luckily my daughter had been showed the same picture in her art lesson to sketch so was able to answer confidently. I made a note of that so your child will be prepared too.

General knowledge is a big thing in private schools. I personally don't allow my daughter to listen to the news because it is so tragic and filled with wars, terror and stuff that my eleven year old doesn't need to be concerned with. They should call it bad news. When my daughter was in year 2, I couldn't understand why the children had a lesson on general knowledge but learned why when she was in year 5. They knew that it would come in handy during interviews.

If you're like me and don't allow your child to watch or read the news then look out for a publication called First News for kids. It's sensitive to children and has a lot of feel good stories. Another idea is to go online to Amazon and purchase a book on General knowledge. The teachers at my daughter's private primary school use one called "Flip Quiz", which are really a lot of fun. They cover Math, Geography, Science and the natural world, History and a bunch of up to date general knowledge that's probably only useful for interviews and games. But the kids love them! So, "Flip Quiz" is definitely worth the purchase.

Please inform your child who the Prime Minister is. I have a funny little story. As I said I personally don't let my daughter watch the dreadful news because I don't want to pollute her mind with tragedy. That's just me. But, I should have at least filled her in on who the Prime Minister is. She was nine at the time when her teacher had asked her who the Prime Minister was. Her answer was David Beckham! Lol. She said her teacher looked at her in shock and pure annoyance. I thought it was funny because I have a sense of humor but her teacher didn't. I read her displeasure in my daughter's school report. It was also at that time that I realized the importance of children having a bit of general knowledge. It will empower them for their interviews.

If you find that your child is still filled with anxiety about interviews, then do get in touch and book in a consultation with me as soon as possible so we can discuss the issue. I believe that outside support can be beneficial. You can reach me at **goodmumsguide@gmail.com**

STEP 9: TIME FOR THE HOLIDAYS

"Bah!" said Scrooge. "Humbug!" - Charles Dickens

As you've probably noticed this step is nearing the end of the journey. You will have done everything necessary to help your child prepare for the big days that lie ahead. If you haven't made your final decisions on the schools you want to apply to, then this really is it. Do it now so you can leave the stress of all that paper work behind. At this point in the game your child needs you more than ever. Halloween is nearing and Father Christmas will be here soon! Every child will be excited to go to winter parties and will be planning on buying their BFF a present with their pocket money. Please don't start calling off all the fun. Some of the parents I know were adamantly against play dates and parties during the lead up to exams. I do not recommend this. It will place too much pressure on your child. We all need to blow off steam and that includes children. So ease up and allow them some fun.

Don't panic if you get a letter in the mail from a school reminding you that your child will be sitting their first exam in October. You will have been made aware of this when you were looking up the admission criteria at the schools you were interested in or you will have received a letter informing you of how the exam process works.

If your child is taking an exam in October then it's really important that you slow down the private tuition to only once a week and that's if it's still necessary. If you feel that enough is enough then end the tutoring two weeks before their exam. This will allow your child to chill and rest up for the big day. Rest and relaxation is so important right now. My daughter was excited for her October exam because it signified to her that primary school was nearly over. She was one of three girls taking early exams so they were able to share their experience with classmates. I think it also gave her confidence for her exams in January.

Remember step three, All You Need Is Love? Well you are going to have to refer to that step and give even more hugs and cuddles with buckets of praise now. They've done the hard work and now is the time for more cuddles and support. A word of advice, try to avoid talking about the exams unless your child wants to. If your son or daughter feels the need to do a bit more revision, then by all means be supportive but don't push. A few days before the exam check to see what they will need to bring to the exam and make sure it's put together, with a bottle of water, near the front door.

The night before the exam make sure they get in bed much earlier because they might find it difficult to get to sleep. Tell your child that you are so proud of all the effort he/she has put in. Tell him/her that you know they are ready and to enjoy the process. When I said this to my child you should have seen her little face light up. Children need to hear that we think they are awesome. So shower your child with praise. I told my daughter it didn't matter what the outcome was because no matter what happened I knew she was an incredible individual. She had worked so hard and that made her a winner to me. I will never forget all the love she showered on me for showering her with love. Please do the same.

For others who are not having exams until January then you should spend about six weeks to do some final tweaks. You can download papers and start timing your child as if they are in the exam. Some children still don't have a sense of time at 10 years old, so would do well to get a feel for the pace they should be working at in order to finish a paper in 1 ½ hours. Make sure you print out more of the past exam papers from the schools of your choice for your child to work through.

If it is clear to you that your child is ready then spend time on the interview project making it spectacular.

Children that are going for scholarships may be given a brief on what is expected and what to prepare for. In art they could be given instructions for a project that they will need to bring in, either before or after the entrance exams, so have them work on making it awesome.

If your child has a music or drama scholarship audition, then spend time preparing the pieces he/she will be expected to perform or the monologue they have to deliver. If you can get family around to listen or watch then that is invaluable. They get to feel the adrenalin as if in the exam environment but with the love energy from family and friends.

If your child is going for a sports scholarship try out, then get him/her in the gym or running on the track to build up their stamina. Get your daughter in the pool to do laps or your son on the tennis court to hit more balls. Success leaves clues. If you ask a successful athlete or musician what made them the best, they will always say it was the time they spent putting into being the best, and that's called practice.

Olympic medalist Jennifer Stoute didn't start running track until she was eighteen, and four years later she ran for Great Britain in her first Olympics in Seoul, Korea in 1988. Four years later in 1992 she won Bronze in the 400m Relay. When I asked her what got her to the Olympics she told me it was hard work. If you ask my daughter how she was able to go from Grade 1 to Grade 5 on piano in two years she will say, "I practiced ninety minutes a day". So, get that last bit of practice in because the time is nigh.

The weeks before Christmas should be enjoyed. If you feel your child needs a bit more time practicing for the exam then go for it; but whatever you do, let them have a break at least a week before Christmas. To be honest, you are going to need a break to chill too, so go a little easy on them.

Why not bake some ginger bread or do a bit of shopping with your child. Whatever you choose to do during this time please don't forget to have some fun. Balance is key. I gave my daughter a special Christmas break with loads of good eating and presents. She deserved it and so does your child. No "bah humbug!" allowed.

STEP 10: THE FINAL FRONTIER

"Children are happy because they don't have a file in their minds called "All the Things That Could Go Wrong." - Marianne Williamson

I love the above quote because children aren't bogged down with the things that can go wrong. They simply do what they do and wait for the result. Now don't get me wrong, in this instance a child might be concerned with how well they do but that is primarily because we are making it into a big deal. We, meaning the teachers and parents, are the ones most concerned with all the things that can go wrong. I know my daughter well enough that if I hadn't made the exam results so important, then she would not have had little wobbles during the lead up to her exams. It's easy for me to say this in hindsight but it's true. Kids just don't stress about stuff like we do. They are pretty much easy going creatures. I love their nature. And it's that very nature that we adults strive for when we are in a yoga class learning to move into the childhood pose. It's the concern of the outcome that makes us so stiff.

Anyway, you are at Step 10 and it is my favorite of all the steps because it is the end of the journey to getting your lovely son or daughter into a top school! You should be excited.

It's January, your child can do no more but wait for exam day. Undoubtedly you will be the one who is most nervous the closer it gets to the exams. Try to hold it together for your child's sake because there is nothing you can do. Remember if you are cool, then your child will show up to the exam in a positive state. State of mind is everything. Please don't be the parent that gets their child all in a frazzle the night before exams. That's so un-cool.

A nice meal the night before and a favorite treat for dessert should be on the menu. How about getting yourself up early on exam day to make home-made pancakes or your child's favorite breakfast. I did that and by doing so you help your child to relax. I even let my daughter watch her favorite cartoons so she didn't have a moment to feel any nerves she might otherwise have experienced. Don't ask your child, "are you nervous?" That could actually make them nervous! Just chill.

It's been an incredible journey to get your precious child this far. A journey that has been filled with a lot of emotion, maybe of your own childhood or possibly you're a single parent and the strain of doing it on your own has been challenging. I have been in your shoes and this is why I wrote this guide because no one else had written anything that would have helped me through it all. I can say with hand on heart that helping your child stand a chance of getting a place in a top school is so rewarding, not just for you but for me as well.

When my daughter entered her school and was given her uniform to put on so we could take pictures of her, I felt like I could finally take a deep breath because it was at that moment it all made sense. All the hours supporting her through her piano lessons, the time spent helping her in all areas of her curriculum, plus the mess in the flat from all the art supplies strewn everywhere, was worth it. She had gained offers from three top schools and earned two art scholarships. Sometimes it wasn't easy, yet at other times it was a lot of fun. I know when you look back on this experience you will see it the same. We got to the final step and you are here now so well done! You and your child are bright twinkling stars in the universe! I am really happy for you.

On the day of the exam give your child a hug and tell him/her to enjoy it. I know that sounds weird, like who enjoys taking an exam right? To your child what they are hearing is "I believe in your ability" and that goes a long way as they answer questions on an exam paper. I like to think my daughter felt like I was right there by her side.

I could go on an on some more but you have stuff to do. I have faith in your ability and anyone who bought this book because you have taken the first step toward getting your child into a top school.

So, good on you and go for it! Please email me and tell me how things are going. I really want to know. You can do so on **goodmumsguide@gmail. com.**

Take care and enjoy the journey.

KK Harris

WHERE DO WE GO FROM HERE?

1. I've given you the ten steps and now it's up to you to implement them. Put together a plan and work through it. Working from a plan is imperative and it will help you to stop feeling overwhelmed.

2. Take one day at a time. Be consistent and celebrate achievements.

3. If it's all too much then hire me as your educational consultant. I would have loved to have had someone to meet with to help me put a plan in place and help me stay focused and on track. Let me manage the process by guiding you every step of the way. I will create a bespoke plan of action specific to your child's needs. Please get in touch at **goodmumsguide@gmail.com** I'm here to help.

The following are a few interviews that I believe will be informative and enjoyable.

INTERVIEW OF OLYMPIAN AND BRONZE MEDAL WINNER JENNIFER STOUTE

Jennifer Stoute is an Olympian twice! In 1988 she represented Great Britain in Seoul and in 1992 in Barcelona, where she won bronze in the 4x400m relay. Jennifer is also a mother of two daughters Alicia and Renee. Her eldest, Alicia is fourteen and is following in her footsteps as a young athletics star for Great Britain.

I had the pleasure of interviewing her and wanted to share it with you. Jennifer is an incredible woman with drive and commitment with a sparkle in her eyes and a smile that makes you want to sit and talk for hours. Unfortunately, I didn't get hours for the interview. Jennifer squeezed me in, between the school drop off and a 9 am meeting.

Ten minutes early I sat waiting for Jennifer to join me for our interview. I had my notes ready because over the years of seeing her at the school front door with promises of coffee that never came into fruition, I knew I had to be prepared. Plus I only had thirty minutes for the interview. Reading over my notes, wearing my navy blue Hollister v-neck and matching yoga trousers (picking cat hairs off my sleeve) I saw her walking through the door greeting me before she got to the table. She wore a big smile that literally lit up the room. I suddenly felt under dressed, less fit, and short.

Jennifer is tall, as in 5'10 with the longest legs to die for. Not only that but she is incredibly fit. I doubt she has more that 5% fat on her lean body. She has the loveliest dread locks cut into a well, manicured bob. Her dress sense is superb and she always looks great. Today is no exception. She's wearing a tight black mini-skirt with black opaque tights and a pair of Gucci loafers. Her blouse is beautiful yet simple in a gorgeous pristine white cotton. She has topped the look with a coat that I swear is by Zadig & Voltaire, but I'm not here to ask her where her wardrobe comes from, so I abstain.

Her energy is infectious and people are staring. A forty something year old guy sitting a table behind her says quietly "that's Jenny Stoute". I want to jump up and say, "yes she is and I'm interviewing her!" She doesn't seem to hear him probably because she is focused on her order, which is a glass of water and toast to take away. I so want a coffee, but like a teenager I want to do what the popular girl is doing, so I order a glass of the clear stuff too.

Jennifer sits down and I'm raring to go. I ever so quickly look at her hair and smile. Like a mind reader, she tells me she's embracing her grey hair with pride. Jennifer celebrated her 50th birthday in April and there is not a sign of wrinkles on her face that would make her consider Botox or fillers. Clearly, her lifestyle of being caffeine and alcohol free, plus her daily work-outs, keep her looking amazing. I suspect it's her can-do-anything attitude that helps regenerate her caramel colored freckled skin.

KK: Hi Jenny, thank you so much for getting together with me on this. It might go out as a pod cast, I hope you don't mind that?

JS: (giggles) No I don't mind that.

KK: You were in the Olympics in 1988 can you tell me about that.

JS: My first Olympics was in 1988 in Seoul with Flo Jo and Dwayne Johnson ran the most incredible 100m that anybody would ever experience, I was there for that. Then in 1992 Barcelona Olympics getting the Bronze medal was a fantastic experience for me at 27 years old. I wasn't a naturally talented youngster but I worked really hard to get to where I was. So for me the highlight of actually getting a medal was amazing.

KK: I can only imagine standing up there on the podium right? That's incredible. What do you think it took to become an Olympian?

JS: You know, I think it takes a lot of drive and determination. I think that as I watch my daughter who is fourteen now, and what she's about, and how she gets from A to B in her life. She sets her goals and these are the goals that she wants. Somewhere between teenager, young kids to adults we seem to lose that whole ability to be focused. What it takes for the young kids is to stay focused. It's about conditioning and repeating. You don't have to be the world's most talented but you have to be a hard worker.

KK: Fantastic. That leads me onto another question. Was it something that you set your eye on as a child?

JS: Yes, in 1984 one of my school friends made the Olympic games in Los Angeles.

KK: My hometown.

JS: (ha-ha) I said to myself "I'd love to go to the Olympics." And everyone said, "there's no way!" I was always last in sport. I was always behind. But I set myself a goal and gave myself four years. I said I'm going to go to the next Olympic games and I made the relay team.

KK: Wow

JS: Its just determination and hoping everything was going to go in my direction.

KK: That just sounds so exciting to me. How old were you when you started track?

JS: I didn't start track until I was eighteen when I came here from Barbados. I was about twenty-three when I went to Seoul and twenty-seven when I went to Barcelona. I didn't start running until quite late. I didn't really do any of the junior championships or any of the step-ups. I just went straight into the seniors.

KK: I didn't have this question written down, but for you to do something like that at eighteen were you just a natural athlete? Were you running around all the time playing as a child?

JS: Yes, I have five brothers. I was always very active. I was always very focused within myself. I didn't have a need for my parents to take me everywhere; it was always me waking myself up to go to school and training. I was focused on myself.

KK: You were like that before eighteen.

JS: Yes.

KK: How early do you think a child should work on becoming a top athlete? You mentioned that your daughter is an athlete already.

JS: When you look at the greats, you see, I think it's all about expectations. Every parent wants their child to be amazing, but if there is a natural ability that you can see and a drive that you can see, then say, put it like this, I have two daughters and one is naturally athletic and she's ten but not focused. My eldest daughter is 14 and very focused. I started her doing drills at 10 or 11. The reason I started her doing this is because she was becoming a bit weighty, you know putting on weight, so I was conscious of it. I wanted her to understand about looking after her body and herself as an individual. From when I started drilling I got her a coach and she was doing drills for a year and a half and she fell in love with track and field. And now she is a 5'8'" slender girl who's very on her track & field. Surprising to both John and I she is now ranked #1 in the country. It's shocking but the advantage that she has is that it's all down to her own inner drive. As a parent it's easy to step into their dream, but you can't. You can give them advice but it has to be their drive.

KK: That's right.

JS: Alicia, every night before she goes to bed she does fifty sit ups, a plank for one minute, and does another exercise without being prompted.

KK: I have to tell you that when you told me that Alicia does fifty sit-ups every night. I started it, and I've been doing them every day for the past few months consistently and I've have to tell you that I've never had this stomach in my life.

JS: See, what it is that she's shown me is that it's just consistency. With children when you see their ability, first you get them involved in all sports and then you can pin point exactly what it is that they can do at an older age. Just get them involved and encourage them. You can pick out the excellence once they get to a certain age.

KK: So your daughter didn't go for a sports scholarship?

JS: No. And the reason why is because the school that we went for at the time didn't have a sports scholarship. It's more of an academic school.

KK: So why did you choose that school?

JS: I chose the school because I love the school itself. I loved how the children were. They were so polite and I like the way they carried themselves. For me the sporting element for Alicia is like a second home. That's my job. That's what I do so she's always going to be involved in that sporting arena. So for me it was the academic side. If she decides to go to university we may go the scholarship route.

KK: To America?

JS: ha-ha, yes maybe, maybe. With my younger daughter Renee, it's going to be interesting to see where she goes.

KK: Can you tell me a little bit about what you do because you mentioned, "this is my job. This is what I do".

JS: What I do is I'm a sports agent/manager. What we do is we manage sports individuals, track & field. We do their races, commercial outlets, their shoe contracts and their sponsorships. What we basically do is create their lifestyle for them. We put them in races throughout the whole of Europe. We have a lot of overseas athletes from America and the Caribbean who spend the whole of three months traveling from airport to airport, going from one track meet to the next. So we organize all of that so they can focus on performing to the best of their ability getting ready for World Championships, Olympic games and European Games.

KK: And what's the name of your company and where is it?

JS: It's called Stellar Athletics and we are based in Connaught Square. We are part of Stellar Football Agency. We look after Gareth Bell, Peter Crouch, and a number of others. We are one of the biggest football agencies around.

KK: I was going to ask if your daughters would follow in your footsteps but I kind of suspect that at least one of them will.

JS: ha-ha

KK: So their father, I didn't want to bring it up. But I think he's incredible.

JS: No it's fine.

KK: Great! I think it's something for the people to know. I see him periodically at the school door, so I know he's very active in their lives. Please tell us who is their father is?

JS: He is John Regis, the British record holder in the 200 meters. He ran it in 20 seconds and no one has done that yet. He ran that in 1997. We both run our business together, which is extraordinary!

KK: I wanted to bring that up because I think it's important. I think parents should represent how it can work. My ex-husband and I still work together as a team raising our daughter.

JS: It's fundamentally important. I come from a divorced family. My parents divorced when I was five years old and it was very dysfunctional, especially when you have parents that don't communicate with each other. And the kids unfortunately become the ones that have to be able to find out through their personality and feelings how to make the best of what's going on. What we have to appreciate is that children don't understand how they feel. So it's important for the adults to keep things as normal as possible for the children. It doesn't matter what's going on in your life because children do not have the ability and growth to understand their feelings. They'll switch from one thing to the next. It's up to the parents to make sure the children are unscathed. Yes there are going to be times when they are hurting and you'll have to sit down to discuss it. They have to have their father in their life.

KK: You are such an inspiration, I mean even just sitting here and learning more about how you run your life and the children's lives and I hope it really inspires others because I think it's really important, especially in this day and age we are living in right now.

JS: It's so easy to attack (referring to ex-husband). I'm not saying I'm an angel and there are times when I just want to lash out and say 'why is my life like this?' but you get to a stage when you say you've got children and they are your responsibility. It's your responsibility to enable them to go out and handle society. What we have to do is give them coping skills, which are fundamental, more than anything in the whole entire world. If you can't educate your children to handle things then they are already going to be on a bad footing in the world of normal kids.

KK: I think your daughters are going to be fine (both giggle).

JS: I think you are amazing. How you told me how you got her into the scholarships and schools.

KK: Thank you very much.

JS: You've used the system to the best of your ability, which is great, whereas me, I had no clue. I've probably done it the most expensive way. If I could have done it any other way, for sure 100% I would have done it the way you have.

KK: You know, when your back is against the wall, what do you do? I'm a fighter and this is why I wrote the book because I know there are a lot of people out there that just don't have a clue, money or not. They don't have a clue on what it takes to get your child into a top school. The consistency that's needed, the commitment from the parent and this is really what I'm trying to get across in the book. The consistency, the commitment, and really knowing your child and what is a good school for your child is important.

KK: Another question is advice to parents who want their child to apply for a scholarship in sports. How many days a week do you think a child should practice their sport? How many days a week is Alicia out there on the track?

JS: Alicia is on the track twice a week.

KK: Really, Is that it? She's the number one in the country.

JS: On a Tuesday and Saturday. What you have to do is look at all the sport they are already doing. She is really active and so you have to look at volume of what your child is doing. I can't add any more time on her time. You have to look at her schedule and then go from there. If your child is doing a specialized sport like Tennis or Golf then you have to add accordingly to what is needed for that sport/event. What you don't want to do is press, because kids have so much going on with homework and all this other stuff. The level of requirement of what they need to do will be depended on how much activity they do throughout the whole week. And then you add on what is needed for that particular sport.

KK: Wow, I would have thought they would have to do their sport everyday. So, that's good information to parents who are thinking how they are going to do it with everything else their child has going on throughout the week.

KK: So how many hours is she training during the week?

JS: Ninety minutes on Tuesday and ninety minutes on Saturday.

KK: Is that with you or with her dad?

JS: John and I have nothing to do whatsoever with her training. We got her a coach and she's with a training group. It's very difficult for us because we are in the industry. We jump on any talented, great kid, but what we've found is that this has allowed her to grow. She has a determination. She knows what she wants. So we allow her to see where she goes from there.

KK: So tell me she's number one for her age group in the country. You and John don't coach her. She has her own coach and training group.

JS: Yes that's right. We drive down to Lee Valley, which takes about 1-½ hours. She does her homework in the car while we're driving down. We don't get back until 9pm at night. She has her own coach and training group, which we think it's important because it allows her to get on with it, and then come back and talk with us about any concerns, like if she feels something is not right with her training. We don't want to be in her face. It's important to have that separation. Last year (2014) she was ranked number one and number two in the 100meters, which blew us away. This year she is in the Under 15's and ranked number three and we'll see where she finishes at the end of the year. The girls she's running against are two years older. She's determined to have a successful year. She has her goals. She has the pedigree to be the best but it has to be her goals. So we'll see where she going to go.

KK: Has Alicia talked about a dream of going to the Olympics for Great Britain?

JS: Yes. She wants a goal. John and I both have Bronze medals. People have asked her if she is intimidated by what we've achieved and her response is "No" because we didn't achieve a Gold medal. She isn't bothered by the fact that she is Jenny Stoute and John Regis's daughter. She's just focused on herself.

KK: That's so incredible and I'm so excited for her. I have to tell you that my daughter Ty is inspired by her and goes to the gym three days a week and works out because she see's how Alicia transformed herself.

JS: I've taught my daughter from a young age the importance of understanding her body type and the importance of exercise and she's transformed from a weighty pre-teen to a 5'8" size 8 teen whose fit and strong. It's not from my doing. She's a very healthy eater as well. She looks after what she's about.

KK: The last question I'd like to ask is what advice would you give parents who are aiming to put their child forward for a sports scholarship? I wrote in the book that these scholarships are about excellence. I know what it took for my daughter to achieve offers of two scholarships from two different schools and just like your daughter the child works consistently. I don't have to tell her anything.

JS: That's the difference see. We have to manage our expectations. We may believe that our child is amazing but we have to be honest we know excellent and we know great. There is a gap between the two. If your child is excellent at something and you believe they have a chance at getting a scholarship then go for it. Sort out all the information you need to get them at the level they need to be and then you look at the school and see what the criteria is to put your child forward for a scholarship. What you have to do is be realistic. What you can't do is invent something and expect your child to be like that because then it becomes pressurized. Now if your child is good at what they do and they push for it, then go for it.

KK: My daughter and I took a walk the other day and I asked her how she comes up with these incredible pieces of art. She told me that when she is with her friends and they are walking in the park and her friend is talking about stuff, she says she often looking up and noticing trees and thinking, "I wonder how I can make that tree?" I am in awe of her passion so I told her that "I'm am so happy that you found your passion at such a young age. Keep doing you".

JS: What she has, which is beautiful, is that she see's the world totally differently to all of us and that in itself is amazing, and that is when you see the quality. That is excellence. And that's what a passion or talent is. You do it without breathing.

KK: Thank you so much. You've just been incredible and it's been so nice getting to know so much about your life in a nutshell, in the twenty minutes. It's inspiring. You are a star. And I can't wait to see where your daughter is going to go.

JS: Nor can I, Thank You.

Interview of Kanako Wakatsuki

As a soloist, chamber musician and a dedicated teacher, Kanako is actively performing and teaching both in Japan and UK. She has performed at numerous venues including The Pump Room, Bath, The Old Hall at Lincoln's Inn, and St James's Piccadilly. Kanako continues to take part in numerous music festivals including public and private concerts. Her repertoire varies in a wide range from Baroque to Modern, but she is particularly fond of music by J.S.Bach. She was a successful participant in the International J.S.Bach Competition in Leipzig in 2006.

Having studied at Toho Gakuen School of Music, Tokyo, and the Royal College of Music, London, her musical achievement was led by Masako Matsuda, Nobuyoshi Kato, the late Yonty Solomon, Andrew Ball, and Simon Nicholls. She has also worked with renowned pianists such as John Lill, Sergey Dorensky, Karl-Heinz Kammerling, and James Lisney in Master classes. She has also received guidance from Julian Jacobson, Ruth Nye, Itzak Rashkovsky (vl.), Richard Deakin (vl.), Koichiro Harada (vl.), and Louise Hopkins (vc.) in Chamber music approach.

In recent years Kanako is kept busy as a teacher too. Between 2003 and 2013 she held a position of a visiting piano teacher at a private school in London. She also regularly accompanies young talented musicians in exams, auditions, and concerts and enjoys sharing her passion for music with them. (**http://www.kanakowakatsuki.com/Profile/profile.html**)

KK: Hi Kanako. Thank you for the interview. How many students over your teaching career have you taught?

KW: Wow I've never really counted. I'm not sure.

KK: Can you guesstimate?

KW: I'd say about 100.

KK: Wow that's fantastic, so you have a lot of experience (Giggles). So you are perfect for this question. Can you tell me how many children you've helped prepare for scholarship auditions over your career?

KW: For the scholarship auditions? Not that many, definitely under ten.

KK: Really. Why do you think that is?

KW: Because it's not easy. For most secondary schools they require Grade 4 or Grade 5 by the age of ten or eleven, and that is not easy to achieve.

KK: What goes in to preparing a child for a music scholarship?

KW: Dedication. Support from parents and focus from the child really.

KK: Do you think that a child has to be naturally gifted in piano or do you think it's just based on dedication?

KW: I think it mostly comes from dedication. Obviously, some talent would help but it's like sport, 90% of it needs to come from the work and practice.

KK: Out of the 100 students that you've taught and the small number of children going for scholarships what do you think hinders the rest from being able to go for scholarships? It's not easy I know, but what is it from your experience that hinders them?

KW: To be honest it's support from the parents. Not just financially. It's the parents that really support their child to practice daily and are interested in what their child does that makes a huge difference:

KK: That says a lot because I know as a parent who has recently gone up for scholarships, I say that the dedication has really been tremendous and I'm glad you agree (ha-ha).

KK: Can you tell me; is it important for the parent to be present when the child is practicing?

KW: It helps. Maybe you don't need to be there all the time but for example when a child comes back from a lesson, then the mother or father should ask, "what did you do today or what did you learn? Or did you get a new book or do you like this piece?" This will show your interest. You need to be their number one fan. As a parent, you need to make sure your child practices every day. You have to tell them to go and sit at the piano and practice for half and hour or one hour. You don't need to be there all the time but you must be aware of what your child is doing.

KK: I think that's great advice. For a child that is aiming to be able to audition for a scholarship, how much time do you think a child will need to practice daily to reach the level required by schools?

KW: Practicing everyday is a must. When you are playing at a high level like Grade 4 or Grade 5 then the pieces are more difficult so practicing a minimum of one hour or more is essential because they'll also be preparing for exams. So, the more time the better.

KK: With my daughter, as you know because you are her teacher, I was right there with her putting in 1-½ hours as she practiced. I was there cooking or cleaning or doing whatever. She was able to achieve a Grade 5 Merit in such a fast time because of the dedication (it took two years and one month for my daughter to achieve Grade 5 level. With our support anything is possible).

KK: What advice can you give parents that are considering taking on the path of a music scholarship?

KW: Basically you need to make this a routine. Maybe some children don't have the patience to sit for a long time, but you need to set the routine. If your child can't sit for an hour then split the practices into two. Do a thirty-minute session in the day and a thirty-minute session in the evening. You need to work around your child's personality. But you need a routine no matter how busy you are.

KK: Say a family is about to go on holiday, or school ends and they are away for six weeks, do you think it's alright to leave the instrument for six weeks over the summer when aiming for a scholarship?

KW: As a teacher it's always been a pain for me to come back to the lessons after the summer holiday because it's the longest break. It's difficult when a child hasn't touched their instrument for the whole of the holiday because children will forget what they learned. So we always have to go back a repeat what they've already done. So I would say if you have an important exam or audition coming up then I would say stay and have a holiday planned then during term time do more than you usually do so you are very prepared.

KK: What advice can you give a parent that is looking to buy a keyboard because they weren't either ready to commit to buying a piano or they didn't have the space for one?

KW: I would always recommend a piano but if you really can't afford one or don't have the space then I would say it's the touch of the keys that is very important. These days they do have really good keyboards that feel like a real piano. So the touch of the keys is very important. I would say no to those keyboards that you can just put on the desk that has less than eighty-eight keys. That's not really a piano now is it?

KK: No it's not. Could you please give advice to children, budding musicians that really want to push themselves as far as they can.

KW: Being able to play a tune that you like is so much fun, but to get to that level is not easy and not fun actually (we giggle), so you need to be prepared. It's not that, just because you like it, you do it. Most children including myself don't like practicing because that's the hardest part. So, be prepared for that part. Learning music is one of the best ways to see the result of your hard work. When you practice then you get better. It's as simple as that, as long as you have a good teacher. You may feel stressed and you may not like it, but then you get good results if you work hard.

KK: Oh, that's wonderful Kanako. Thank you for giving this interview for the book. I really appreciate it.

If you are considering piano lessons for yourself, son or daughter then please contact Kanako. She gives private lessons from her home in South West London. Please email her at **piano@kanakowakatsuki.com**

INTERVIEW OF OWNERS AND CLINICIANS OF HAMPSTEAD DYSLEXIA CLINIC

I contacted the owners and head clinicians at Hampstead Dyslexia Clinic because I was looking for a clinic to have a client's daughter assessed for Dyslexia. My client wanted an assessment centre that was warm and welcoming and not intimidating like a medical facility. My client was extremely happy with the service they received at Hampstead Dyslexia Clinic so I knew I had to interview the owners for this book.

I fell in love with the story of Renee Lawton-Browne, the original owner of Hampstead Dyslexia Clinic and mother of a Dyslexic son. It was her love for her child that gave her the impetus to find a way for him to reach his full potential.

As a teacher and deputy head of the primary school her son attended, Renee suggested that they should create a program for students with Dyslexia. Although the school was sympathetic, they said that because the condition was not well known, at the time, then they couldn't get the funding to support the program. So what was a mother to do? She re-trained and opened her own clinic, which is the Hampstead Dyslexia Clinic where she taught and had a staff of over twenty-five helping to bring a love of learning and understanding to hundreds of Dyslexic children and their families. When her daughter Delia graduated from university she went straight into training to be a clinician and to work at the clinic with her mother. Her mother passed away in July 2008 but her legacy continues through the work of her daughter and son in law, Seth and Delia Gasgoigne.

I had the opportunity to have an hour of their time, although Delia had to step away to teach half way through the interview, Seth carried on. Both are passionate about what they do and the children and adults that come to them seeking answers. Answers to questions about why they can't spell or write or do maths like everybody else. Both Seth and Delia opened my eyes wider to Dyslexia and how the Hampstead Dyslexia Clinic has helped individuals for over thirty years gain confidence where it was once lost.

I have a twin- brother who has Dyslexia and it was not easy for him growing up during a time when there was not a known name for the way he processes information. As you can imagine I have a soft spot for anyone that has Dyslexia.

I was nearly brought to tears at times during the interview as I listened to them recount how relieved parent's and students are when they have a diagnosis. I guess it brought back a lot of memories of my childhood. My twin-brother finally got his diagnosis in his twenties. He now lives a much happier life and is pursuing the dreams he only dreamed of as a child.

I hope that this interview will bring you some understanding of Dyslexia. If you think your child may be Dyslexic please be encouraged to get in contact with Hampstead Dyslexia Clinic, London.

KK: Hi Delia and Seth, thank you for taking the time out of your schedule to do this interview. I'm going to jump right in. Are schools required to recognize Dyslexia as a condition?

SG: Yes there is legislation that requires schools to acknowledge the condition. The problem is that particularly state schools, budgets are stretched and they only have a certain amount of funds available to use to support their children with Dyslexia.

KK: Isn't the Pupil Premium being utilized for the extra support needed for students with Dyslexia? (Pupil Premium is additional funding for publicly funded schools in England to raise the attainment of disadvantaged pupils and close the gap between them and their peers. **https://www.gov.uk/pupil-premium-information-for-schools-and-alternative-provision-settings)**

SG: The issue with the Pupil Premium is that it's not exclusively used for a student with Dyslexia or there are students that fall through the gaps because they haven't been diagnosed and don't get to benefit from the support being offered. To make matters worse, getting a diagnosis through the system can take six months or even more.

KK: That leads me to the question: How is Dyslexia assessed?

DG: Some schools will do screeners like the GL Assessment's Special Educational Needs (SEN) screener. Which might not come up or come up mild or moderate. The problem is that it doesn't test memory, which is a massive component. It's looking at phonological awareness, it's looking at Rapid Naming. It does look at some of the key aspects that are the foundation pillar stones of what people thought Dyslexia was.

SG: However that has been expanded over time. It is no longer just phonics. Unfortunately, some teachers will think that because a child can read well that he/she isn't Dyslexic. We now know that not to be the case. It can be to do with processing or memory and a number of many areas.

KK: Around four years ago, I was tutoring a girl and what I noticed was that when she was reading a word, say "there", she would come back to the word five words later and it was as if she had never seen the word in her life. It kept happening and I said it wasn't right. I suggested that her parents have her assessed for Dyslexia. The parents said, "No, she's just with the fairies." So never had her tested. The end result is that she had to be tutored four to five days a week just so she could sit entrance exams when she was in year 6.

DG: We've heard very similar stories over the years, which could have been avoided had she been assessed. Saying that, we have found that the screeners that are given has come back to be incorrect. We'd say at least 50% to be incorrect. The parents are unhappy because they know something isn't right with their child.

KK: Mothers intuition I call it.

SG: There is nothing that we tell a parent that they don't already know. They have seen it for themselves day in and day out with their child, from homework at the weekends or when they are reading with them. What we give them is a definition for it.

KK: Do you find that most children with Dyslexia, because of their different way of processing are gifted or phenomenal in different areas?

SG: Yes we do actually. We have children that are exceptional in cricket, comedy, painting, or playing an instrument. (Delia exits the room and returns with a framed photograph of a university graduate)

DG: This is a picture of one of the clinics past students. He came to the clinic when he was around seven years old. (In the mid 80's)

KK: Yes the mullet hairstyle tells me that. (We all laugh)

SG: This is Michael Brown. He was told he didn't have a brain and his diagnosis was that he had moderate to severe dyslexia. One problem today is that people want this quickly. I've had parents say "how can this be solved or how soon 'til it's fixed?" Michael came to the clinic from seven years old until twenty-one. He went on to university, studying Engineering and Mechatronics. His degree was mainly manual, building robots. Rene and Delia helped him with his dissertation. He then went on to do a Masters in Robotics & Automation. He became one of the youngest VP's at British Aerospace. He went into the interview and there were thirty guys from all the universities and they gave them a bunch of parts and said, "What can you do with it?" The others were reading instructions but he couldn't read instructions still. So he just built a robot right there and then. The company hired him because they said they needed people that could build things without instructions and his mind does that. Today he has a start-up where he has invented microscopic windshield wipers for keyhole surgery.

KK: That's really incredible and makes sense.

SG: Instead of taking the keyhole camera out and cleaning it, it's done internally. He tried to explain it to me and it didn't make sense! (Seth laughs at himself) Michael comes to our summer camp every year. He says he still doesn't know his times tables. The children ask how is it that he is an engineer and doesn't know his times tables? His response is that he speaks to Google in his phone and asks questions. He uses technology to help him.

SG: We have a fourteen-year-old girl who can't read or write and has Dyscalculia (difficulty understanding numbers) and as a result can only count in ones, yet she is an incredible cook. She comes up with incredible, wonderful recipes- as good as Jamie Oliver. She makes a delicious Crème Brule, yet she is in the bottom of all of her classes and came to us with very low self- esteem.

KK: How do you help a child like that?

SG: First we start with her self esteem and work on building that up. I asked her to make a recipe. She said she needed a handful of this and a pinch of that. I told her that that wasn't going to help if she was writing a book. She asked me how she was going to do that. I told her get the scale and put that handful into it and write it down. She said "but I can't write". I told her, "put it in your Dictaphone on your mobile phone." I said, "We are going to get your recipe book written". She'll have her own book out one day.

90

KK: With the likes of Amazon she'll be fifteen when it comes out!

KK: I think this is a good time we are living in and it is only going to get better for children with Dyslexia or any other learning disability.

KK: You know, I'm sure my mother was Dyslexic and a few of my other siblings are as well. I'm curious Is Dyslexia genetic?

DG: Yes it is. We know that it is passed down through the father. We always interview the parents to learn more about them and quite often discover that one may not be able to spell properly or is highly disorganized. They have usually gone undiagnosed.

SG: For children that have difficulty reading we even suggest audio books. We have children that listen to the classics and can recite nearly the whole book. It's made it possible for the child to get through a huge selection of books taking the pain that comes from not being able to read like their peers.

KK: What systems are used to teach Dyslexic children at the program here at Hampstead Dyslexia Clinic?

DG: Unlike some other prominent Dyslexia organizations, we don't pre-scribe to a very strict program. I teach as well as our teachers teach in a very multi-sensory way depending on where the child's strengths and weaknesses are. If they are a hands-on learner we tend to go more with that in terms of spelling, and if they are visual we are more than likely going to have them draw a picture or colour code. We also follow the Alpha to Omega program by Beve Hornsby. That's our main program for spelling and for reading. Depending on the child we may also use the Toe-by-Toe method or Tapping Out (tapping out the syllables) or Touch Typing. We find no one system works for all. We employ different styles of learning to each individual.

KK: Let me interrupt. You mentioned Touch Typing, why do you teach that?

SG: It's vital for those that have difficulty with writing because generally they may have difficulty in motor coordination. If they are a slow processor then their writing will be slower so it will help because all they have to do is remember the fingering. If a child has illegible handwriting they may be losing points on exams. Now you can use a computer just as long as you can type as fast as you can write.

(Delia has to go off to teach leaving Seth and I to finish the interview without her)

KK: I see that your laptop is colour coded. Why is that?

SG: On the keyboard the little fingers use the yellow keys, ring fingers are the green keys, middle fingers are the blue keys and you attack the red keys with your other fingers (thumbs and pointing fingers). There is a program we use called Nessy. They do software for children with Dyslexia. They do a learning program, a touch-typing program, a reading program and phonics as well. They are games based.

KK: Are these programs by Nessy accessible to parents or just teachers?

SG: Yes they are accessible to parents. The prices vary from £15 to around £65 per program (check website for details http://www.nessy.com/uk/).

KK: What are Mnemonics?

SG: It's a way to help recall information. By knowing a saying that is associated with the word is helpful when remembering how to spell it. Like take for example the word "very" to recall its spelling we use the Mnemonic, "Vampires Eat Red Yogurt". Quite often a Dyslexic will spell the word "does" as "dus" but by using a Mnemonic they spell it correctly because they can remember "Dogs Often Eat Slugs". There are hundreds of Mnemonics that can help individuals spell, which we utilize. The best Mnemonics are the ones children come up with themselves. Mnemonics can be used for the computer keyboards as well.

KK: I noticed on the website that you will speak with class teachers. How receptive are schools with you coming in and discussing one of their Dyslexic students?

SG: For the most part they are very receptive. I would say the higher achieving the school the less receptive, not across the board, but if your child has gotten into a high achieving school they will assume that you don't have a learning disability. Saying that, the reality is that most schools want their students to do well, so they if a child has been accepted into a top school but still needs that support, then the school will usually do what it takes to make sure the proper support staff is there. At least this is what we've found to be the case.

KK: What is the commitment you expect from the students that attend Hampstead Dyslexia Clinic?

SG: We expect total commitment and will not accept non-attendance for anything other than illness or say a Jewish holiday (we have a lot of Jewish students) for example. It's vitally important that the commitment is made. Children come into the clinic during school times because the school understands that they cannot support them. So they'll see us for their English and Maths lessons.

KK: Do they have to have special permission?

SG: Yes certainly. Quite a number of our students come for lessons during school time. We have lessons for students both children and adults from morning until 9pm at night.

KK: I see you have a summer camp for children. Can you tell me a little about that?

SG: Yes. We have a one-week summer program that Delia put together. It's a fun week where children are engaged in learning in a very fun way. One summer we told them they would be putting together a play and acting it out on video at the end of the week. We took them through the process of mind mapping ideas to come up with characters; through to the development of a script and set design. Those that couldn't write recorded the description of characters into a Dictaphone. We hired in animators to teach the children to turn the play into an animation using Ipads. On day four we had a professional acting coach come in to help them act out a scene. By the end of the week they had a full essay including planning, creation, description, conclusion and a film.

KK: That sounds like so much fun. My daughter would absolutely love it! What I feel from you and Delia is that you both have so much passion for what you do. I've learned so much more about Dyslexia during this interview and I know that I've only scratched the surface. I just want to say thank you for giving up your time so generously.

SG: It's been a pleasure KK.

KK: One final question. Do you have any plans to write a book?

SG: Yes we do. We've been writing for the past year putting together information for parents who would like resources to help them in parenting their Dyslexic Child.

KK: That's great news! There are parents that do want to know about Dyslexia and would welcome a book from you and Delia. I will be happy to share that information to the parents that come to my website. One more time, thank you so much and thank you to Delia.

If you would like your son or daughter to be assessed for Dyslexia please contact either Seth or Delia to arrange an appointment and tell them KK Harris sent you. Their website address is **www.hampsteaddyslexiaclinic. co.uk**

REFERENCES

Amazon.co.uk '11+ Confidence: CEM Style Practice Exam Papers Book 2: Complete With Answers And Full Explanations: Volume 2: Amazon.Co.Uk: Eureka! Eleven Plus Exams: 9781514270226: Books'. N.p., 2015. Web. 20 July 2015.

Bbc.co.uk,. 'BBC - History For Kids'. N.p., 2015. Web. 20 July 2015.

Biography Online,. 'Quotes By Princess Diana ‚Ä¢'. N.p., 2015. Web. 20 July 2015.

BrainyQuote,. 'Confucius Quotes At Brainyquote.Com'. N.p., 2015. Web. 20 July 2015.

Goodreads,. 'A Quote By Abraham Maslow'. N.p., 2015. Web. 20 July 2015.

Goodreads,. 'A Quote By Martha Graham'. N.p., 2015. Web. 20 July 2015.

Goodreads,. 'A Quote From This Day Forward'. N.p., 2015. Web. 20 July 2015.

Hampstead-school-of-art.org,. 'Building On Our Tradition Of Observation Through Drawing, Painting And Sculpture - Hampstead School Of Art'. N.p., 2015. Web. 20 July 2015.

Interwebicly,. '61 Inspirational Marianne Williamson Quotes'. N.p., 2014. Web. 20 July 2015.

Isi.net,. 'Find A Report - ISI - Independent Schools Inspectorate'. N.p., 2015. Web.

20 July 2015.

Nfer.ac.uk,. 'Non-Verbal Reasoning Tests'. N.p., 2015. Web. 20 July 2015.

Nfer.ac.uk,. 'Verbal Reasoning Tests'. N.p., 2015. Web. 20 July 2015.

Quotations, ThinkExist.com. 'Aristotle Quotes'. Thinkexist.com. N.p., 2015. Web. 20 July 2015.

Reports.ofsted.gov.uk,. 'Find An Ofsted Inspection Report'. N.p., 2015. Web. 20 July 2015.

UK, Sumac. 'Russell Group: Home'. Russellgroup.ac.uk. N.p., 2015. Web. 20 July 2015

17999297R00058

Printed in Great Britain
by Amazon